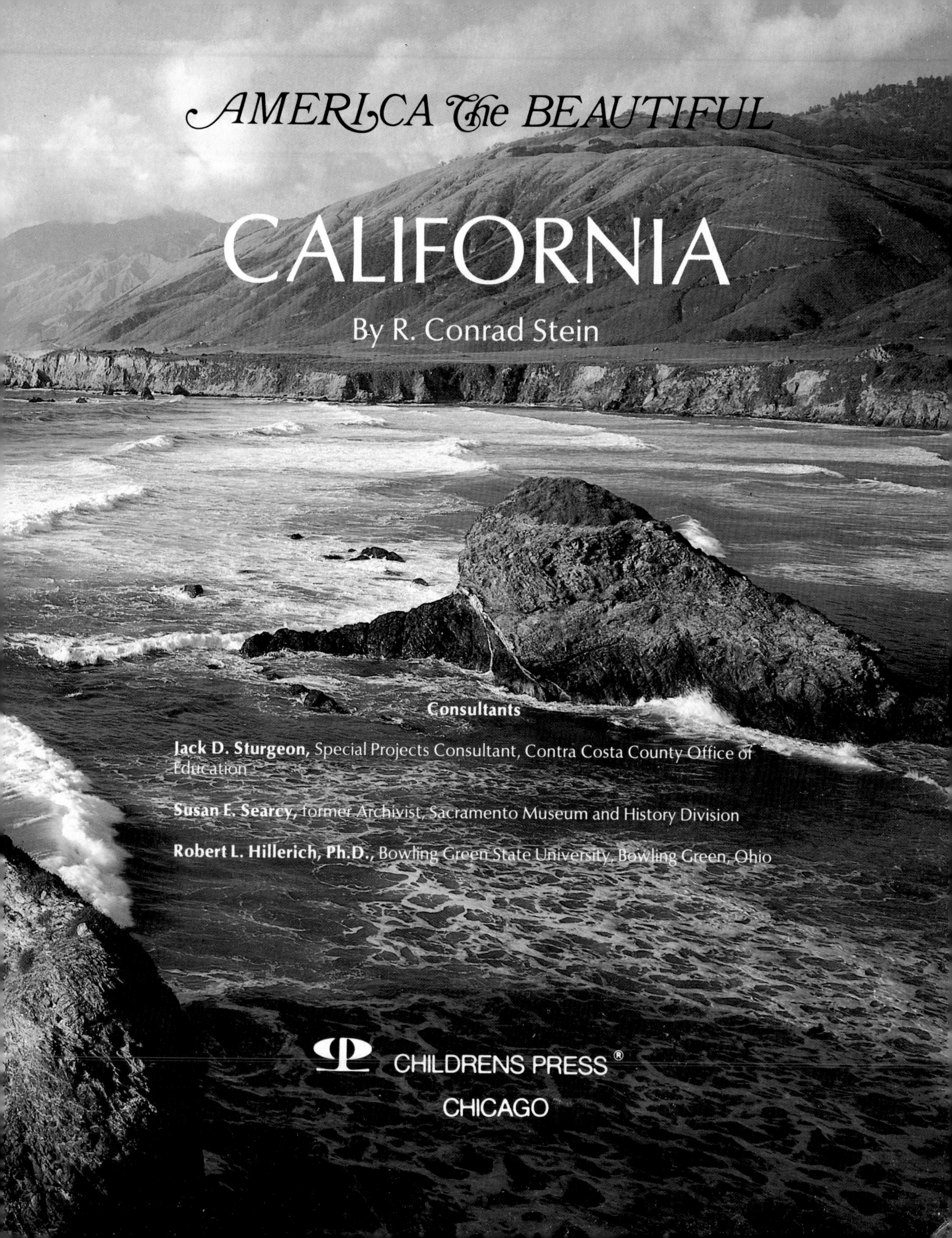

AMERICA the BEAUTIFUL

CALIFORNIA

By R. Conrad Stein

Consultants

Jack D. Sturgeon, Special Projects Consultant, Contra Costa County Office of Education

Susan E. Searcy, former Archivist, Sacramento Museum and History Division

Robert L. Hillerich, Ph.D., Bowling Green State University, Bowling Green, Ohio

CHILDRENS PRESS®

CHICAGO

A San Francisco cable car on the Hyde Street hill

Project Editor: Joan Downing
Assistant Editor: Shari Joffe
Design Director: Margrit Fiddle
Typesetting: Graphic Connections, Inc.
Engraving: Liberty Photoengraving

FOURTH EDITION, 1992.
INCLUDES 1990 CENSUS FIGURES.

Childrens Press®, Chicago

Library of Congress Cataloging-in-Publication Data

Stein, R. Conrad.
    America the beautiful. California / by R. Conrad Stein.
        p.   cm. — (America the beautiful state books)
    Includes index.
    Summary: Introduces the geography, history,
government, economy, industry, culture, historic sites, and
famous people of this beautiful, diverse, and wealthy
Pacific Coast state.
    ISBN 0-516-00451-4
    1. California—Juvenile literature. [1. California.]
I. Title. II. Series.
F861.3.S69   1988   87-37948
979.4—dc19   CIP
                                                    AC

The surf at Balboa Beach

TABLE OF CONTENTS

Chapter 1   An Introduction to the Golden State. 7

Chapter 2   The Land. 9

Chapter 3   The People. 23

Chapter 4   The Beginning. 29

Chapter 5   The World Rushes In. 41

Chapter 6   Building the California Dream. 53

Chapter 7   Government and the Economy. 67

Chapter 8   Arts and Entertainment. 79

Chapter 9   Highlights of the Golden State. 91

Facts at a Glance. 109

Maps. 133

Index. 138

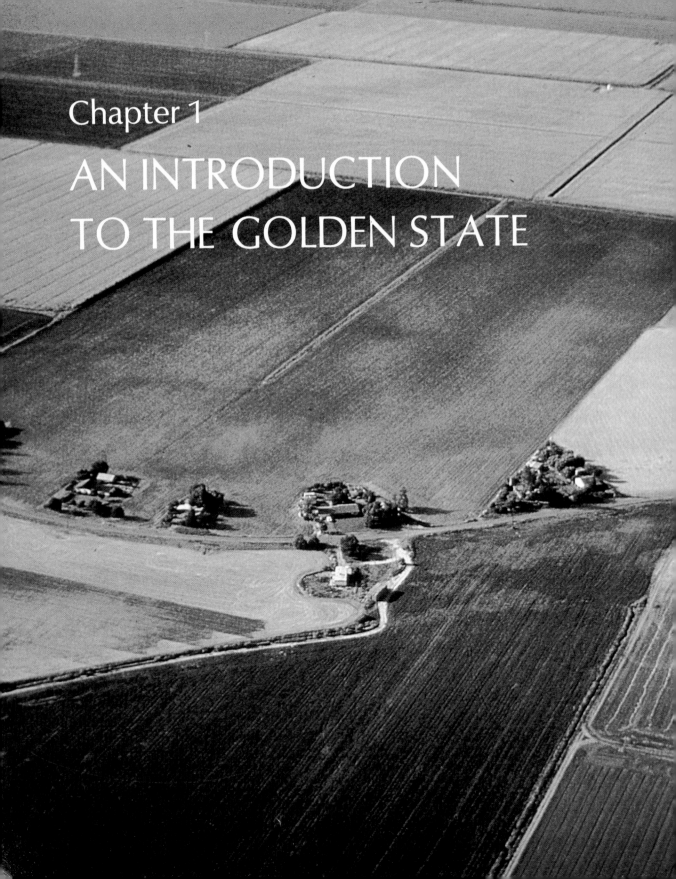

Chapter 1
AN INTRODUCTION
TO THE GOLDEN STATE

AN INTRODUCTION TO THE GOLDEN STATE

For millions of Americans and foreign-born people, California is a golden dream, a place to start life anew. This notion of California as a "promised land" is more than a century old.

In its history as a state, millions of people have flocked to California seeking wealth. At first, land and adventure drew people to the state; then gold; next, rich farmland; and, finally, jobs in commerce and industry. While only a few grew rich, many found a bountiful life in what became known as the Golden State. Even those whose dreams of wealth went unfulfilled were awed by the land around them—trees that pierced the sky like the spires of cathedrals and mighty mountains rising beside lonely beaches.

California pioneers learned that the land could be as generous as it was beautiful. The rich black earth, nourished by the gentle sun, yielded bountiful harvests. The mountains offered a wealth of minerals. California is now the richest of the fifty states. In fact, if California were an independent nation, it would be the world's sixth-most-productive economy. Because this brisk economy has produced numerous jobs, many people have come to the state to find work. One of every ten Americans now lives in California, and since the early 1960s it has been the nation's most-populous state.

Today's California dazzles with natural beauty, culture, economic power, and Hollywood glitter. Yesterday's California is a storybook world of Old West adventure. From every viewpoint, California is, certainly, the Golden State.

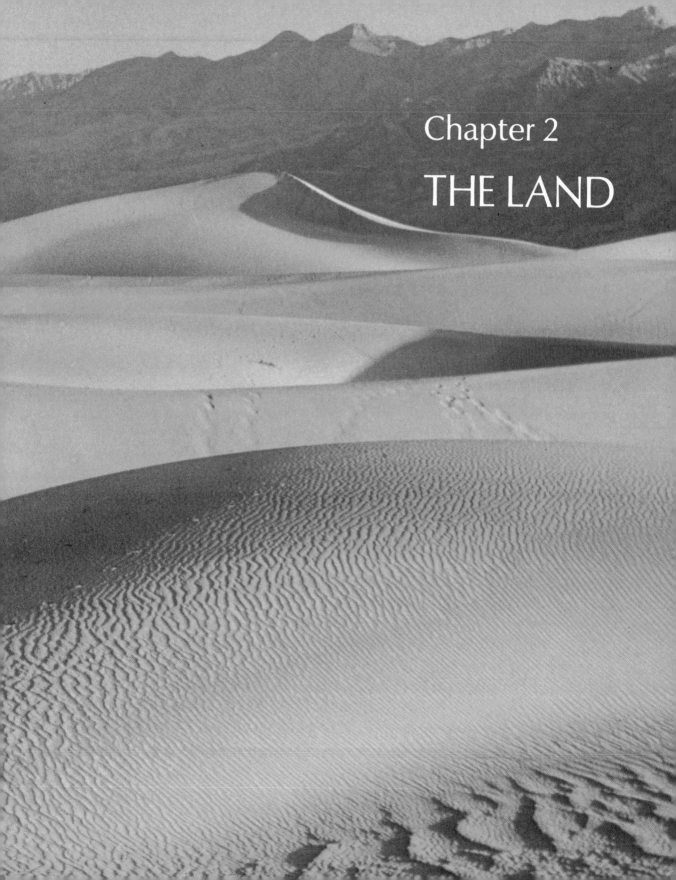

Chapter 2
THE LAND

THE LAND

Everyone needs beauty as well as bread,
places to play in and pray in
where nature may heal and cheer
and give strength to body and soul alike.
                    —John Muir, naturalist

LAND FORMS

Why did the movie industry, early in this century, choose to locate in southern California? The agreeable climate and long, sunny days were not the only reasons; most compelling was the fantastic variety of landscapes offered by the Golden State. Vast deserts to Swiss Alps—a movie company could find either just a few hours away. The sand-swept Mojave Desert and California's snow-covered Sierra Madre Mountains are typical of the extremes of beauty to be found in California.

Mountains and their valleys give California its great physical diversity. The rugged Klamath and Cascade mountains rise in the north. To the south are the Tehachapi Mountains and the gentler Los Angeles and San Diego ranges. California has two mountain "spines" that run north and south through the state. The Sierra Nevadas stand along the state's eastern border, and the Coast Ranges hug the Pacific shore. The Tehachapi Mountains tie the Sierra Nevadas and the Coast Ranges together; many Californians consider the Tehachapis to be the dividing line between northern and southern California.

Beautiful Lassen Volcanic National Park (above) and the fertile Sacramento River delta (right) are two facets of California's varied geographic character.

Sandwiched between the Coast Ranges and the Sierras rests the great Central Valley. It extends about 430 miles (692 kilometers) north to south and averages 50 miles (80 kilometers) east to west. The valley contains some of the richest farmland on earth. The northern portion of the Central Valley is drained by the Sacramento River and is called the Sacramento Valley; the southern portion is drained by the San Joaquin River and is known as the San Joaquin Valley. The Sacramento and the San Joaquin are the Central Valley's primary rivers.

California is home to the highest and lowest points in the continental United States. Mount Whitney, in the Sierras, towers 14,494 feet (4,418 meters) above sea level, while Badwater, at Death Valley in the southeastern desert, plunges 282 feet (86 meters) below sea level. These two extremes, Mount Whitney and Badwater, are little more than an hour's drive apart.

The wide, sandy beaches of the southern California coast give way
to rugged, rocky shores farther north.

GEOGRAPHY

California spreads over 158,693 square miles (411,013 square
kilometers), making it slightly larger than Japan. It ranks third
among the American states in area; only Alaska and Texas are
larger.

California is bordered by Oregon to the north, Nevada and
Arizona to the east, the Pacific Ocean to the west, and the country
of Mexico to the south.

The state's Pacific coastline runs 840 miles (1,352 kilometers),
the longest seacoast of any state except Alaska and Florida. San
Francisco Bay sprawls over 400 square miles (1,036 square
kilometers) and could almost be considered an inland sea. The bay
at San Diego is busy with both commercial and military shipping.
Monterey Bay is steeped in state history.

Two island groups, the Santa Barbara Islands (also known as
the Channel Islands) and the tiny Farallon Islands, are part of
California's territory. The Santa Barbaras lie along the southern
shore and the Farallons dot the waters just west of San Francisco.

Lake Tahoe, in the Sierra Nevada Mountains, is the largest California lake and one of the world's deepest.

RIVERS AND LAKES

The Sacramento and San Joaquin, which move through the Central Valley, form California's largest river systems. Traveling from north to south, the state's other major rivers include the Klamath (and its chief tributary the Trinity), the Mad, the Eel, and the Russian. The Pit, McCloud, Feather, and American rivers are major tributaries of the Sacramento. The Stanislaus, Tuolumne, and Merced rivers link up with the San Joaquin. The Salinas winds through the Santa Lucia Range to empty into Monterey Bay. The Santa Clara and Santa Ana are two major southern California rivers.

California has about eight thousand lakes of various sizes. Lake Tahoe, in the Sierra Nevada Mountains, is the largest California lake and one of the world's deepest. Roughly two-thirds of Lake Tahoe lies in California and one-third lies in Nevada. Clear Lake, Shasta Lake, and Honey Lake are major lakes in the north. There are fewer lakes in southern California as this region of the state receives less rain.

California's climate, as varied as the land itself, ranges from cold, snowy winters in Squaw Valley (left) to warm, sunny weather in Carlsbad (below).

CLIMATE

On New Year's Day, millions of Americans enjoy the Tournament of Roses Parade broadcast from Pasadena in sunny southern California. Tuning in this event allows people from the cold northern states to temporarily tune out the howling winds and deepening snowdrifts. Even though winter is chillier than summer in southern California, some flowers bloom year-round!

But this gentle weather, so envied by people living in harsher climates, is typical only in the narrow belt of land south of San Francisco that lies between the Coast Ranges and the Pacific shore. There, warm Pacific breezes and currents create a "Mediterranean climate," which is characterized by hot, dry summers and rainy or semi-rainy winters. Californians hail this lovely weather as a special gift from nature.

Away from the southern coastal region, California's climate is as varied as the land itself. The deserts of southeastern California can become torrid. In 1913, at Death Valley, the temperature soared to 134 degrees Fahrenheit (56.7 degrees Celsius), the hottest temperature ever recorded in the United States. By contrast, only a day's drive north of Death Valley, the Sierra Mountains can become a winter wonderland. When the 1960 Olympic Games were held at Squaw Valley in the Sierras, there was plenty of snow for the skiers and ice for the skaters. The lowest temperature ever recorded in California was measured in 1937 at Boco, north of Lake Tahoe, where the mercury plunged to 45 degrees below zero Fahrenheit (minus 42.8 degrees Celsius).

With few exceptions, rainfall is far greater in northern California than in southern California. For example, Crescent City in the north is soaked with 80 inches (203 centimeters) of rain a year, while the southern city of San Diego receives only 10 inches (25 centimeters). However, the vast majority of the people and many productive farms are in the southern half of the state. To distribute water from the wet north to the rain-starved south, Californians have built a complex and ingenious system of aqueducts.

THE GREAT WILDERNESS

In 1852, hunter A. T. Dowd came upon a stand of trees so enormous they looked otherworldly. Dowd hiked to a mining camp where the miners laughed at his story and accused him of seeing things that weren't there. Dowd coaxed several men back to the redwood grove and demanded, "Now, boys, do you believe my big tree story?"

Even today, California visitors are astounded the first time they see a grove of redwood trees. Coastal redwoods are the tallest trees on earth, often reaching the height of a thirty-story office building. The redwoods grow close together, and their branches meet and block the sunlight. These magnificent coastal redwoods, which thrive in misty weather, grow only on a narrow strip of land that hugs the Pacific shoreline and extends north from San Francisco to the Oregon border and beyond.

Another magnificent California tree is the giant sequoia. It is closely related to the redwood but grows farther inland. Though giant sequoias are not as tall as coastal redwoods, some have trunks that are thirty feet (nine meters) or more in diameter.

More than 45 percent of California is forestland. Firs and pines are the most common softwood trees. The state is home to several kinds of pine, including ponderosa pine and Monterey pine. Scientists claim that one particular Great Basin bristlecone pine, in the White Mountains of eastern California, is 4,600 years old. This bristlecone pine is the oldest living tree in the world. Cypress trees rise gracefully from the rocky soil along the southern coast. Palms line the streets of San Diego and other cities in the south. In California, the predominant hardwood tree is the oak.

California's nickname, the "Golden State," in part refers to the gold that was once taken from the land in an almost mindless fury. The "Golden State" name was also inspired by the golden grasses that blanket the hillsides in the summer months. Many hills are covered with chaparral—tangles of small trees and shrubs that reach a height of ten feet (three meters) or so. Cowboys of the Old West wrapped their legs with leather "chaps" to protect them from the thorny chaparral branches.

California's forests, grasslands, deserts, coasts, and mountains give refuge to a rich variety of animal life. Coyotes prowl the deserts where rattlesnakes and lizards slide through the sands. Deer, elk, bears, foxes, and wildcats inhabit the forests. Mountain sheep and pronghorned antelope graze the highlands. Ducks, geese, and quail fly overhead. And swimming in the state's rivers and freshwater lakes are salmon, trout, and many types of bass.

California's magnificient coastal redwoods (above) and giant sequoias (right) are the tallest trees on earth. The golden grasses that blanket the hillsides in the summer months (below) were an inspiration for the "Golden State" nickname.

Such sights as El Capitan, on the Merced River (above), and Bridalveil Falls (right) greet visitors to spectacular Yosemite National Park.

THE CONSERVATION MOVEMENT

Shortly after the 1849 gold rush, a young Wisconsin-born man arrived by ship at San Francisco. He asked a passerby the best way out of town.

"Where do you wish to go?" asked the passerby.

"Anywhere that is wild," said the man.

The young man was John Muir, one of America's greatest conservationists. After leaving San Francisco, Muir walked the width of the state until he reached the spectacular Yosemite Valley. He was awestruck by the beauty, and later wrote that the valley was "by far the grandest of all the special temples of Nature I was ever permitted to enter."

But even during Muir's time, the natural wonders of California were being destroyed by a reckless pursuit of money. Mining operations turned sparkling mountain streams into rivers of mud. Logging companies denuded entire groves of redwoods, groves that had taken nature two thousand years to foster. The loggers were so thoughtless that they cut down one-third of California's giant sequoias before realizing that the wood had little commercial value.

Muir was a powerful writer and he published articles drawing attention to the destruction of California's natural resources. Because of his efforts, Congress passed the Yosemite National Park Bill in 1890. To be certain that people would always recognize the need to preserve natural resources, Muir organized the Sierra Club. This group of men and women was dedicated to "preserving the forests and other natural features of the Sierra Nevada Mountains." Today, the Sierra Club is a nationwide organization and a powerful lobby for preservation and conservation.

The confrontations between conservation groups and businesses that wish to develop the land for profit continue. Today, arguments center on such issues as drilling additional oil wells off the coast or on building houses in an undeveloped valley in the south. Over the years, the conservationists have scored some impressive victories, and California has preserved a wealth of national and state parks—for Californians and for posterity.

THE RESTLESS EARTH

On a February morning in 1971, Mrs. Badaloni of the Granada Hills area of Los Angeles awoke when her bed jerked violently. Her mind froze on a single thought: *earthquake*! "My babies! My babies!" she screamed, bolting out of bed. Again the house lurched and Mrs. Badaloni was thrown against the bedroom wall. Finally she managed to collect all her seven children and crawl out of the house. They spent the rest of the morning inside their station wagon, shivering with cold and fright.

Earthquake damage from one of the many tremors that have rattled
Californians over the years

In other sections of Los Angeles, freeway bridges collapsed,
houses crumbled, and windows shattered. The shaking earth
devastated a supermarket so completely that one eyewitness said,
"It looks like what would happen if a jet plane crashed into it."
One of the quake's cruelest strokes occurred at Sylmar, where the
Veterans Administration Hospital caved in and killed forty
patients. In all, sixty-four people died because of the quake.
Property damage was put at $500 million.

The 1971 Los Angeles earthquake was only one of many
tremors that have rattled the people of California. Thirty-eight
years earlier, in 1933, an earthquake struck Long Beach, killing
120 people. The great San Francisco earthquake of 1906 killed 700
people.

Earthquakes stem from fault lines that lie deep below the
surface of the earth. A fault is an ancient break in the earth's crust.
At a fault line, opposing plates of bedrock come together like the
eaves on a slanting roof. When these plates shift—even only a few
inches—the ground above the plates is given a powerful jolt.

The San Andreas Fault stretches from the northern California coast to the Mexican border.

More than a dozen major fault lines crisscross California. The most dangerous is the San Andreas Fault, which stretches 650 miles (1,046 kilometers) from the northern California coast to the Mexican border. It passes through many densely populated areas, including San Francisco and its suburbs. In some places, the San Andreas Fault can be seen from the air—stretching like an open wound across the land. The San Andreas Fault is one of the world's most active fault lines.

No one can predict exactly when the next major earthquake will occur in California, but many scientists believe it will happen before the year 2000. Even so, few people leave the state because they fear impending disaster. Most Californians regard their beautiful land as a gift from nature, not a threat. They would live nowhere else, so they become philosophical about possible dangers. One Californian told a writer, "Earthquakes—why worry? You can get killed a lot quicker on the freeway."

Chapter 3
THE PEOPLE

THE PEOPLE

I like to think how nice it's gonna be, maybe, in California.
Never cold. An' fruit ever' place, an' people just bein'
in the nicest places, little white houses in among the orange
trees. I wonder—that is, if we all got jobs an' all work—
maybe we can get one of them little white houses . . .
—Ma Joad, in John Steinbeck's novel *The Grapes of Wrath*

WHO ARE THE CALIFORNIANS?

During California parties, a common small-talk question is,
"Where are you from?" It seems as though Californians are
always from somewhere else, another state or perhaps a foreign
country. Statistics compiled in 1986 show that 55 percent of the
state's residents were born outside the state. But this is not new.
Will Rogers, the beloved comedian of the 1930s, once entertained
a meeting of The Old Settlers of California. Rogers wrote, "No one
was allowed to attend unless he had been in the state at least two
and a half years."

California enjoys a rich racial and ethnic mix; according to the
1990 census, 69 percent of the population is white, 7.4 percent
black, 9.6 percent Asian, and 13.2 percent of the population
classify themselves as "other." California's Native Americans
number 242,164, comprising .8 percent of the state's total
population. Oklahoma is the only state with more Native
Americans than California.

Hispanics and Asians are the state's fastest growing ethnic

Olvera Street, in downtown
Los Angeles, is lined with
Mexican shops and restaurants.

groups. Hispanics, who can be of any race, make up 25.8 percent
of California's population, and more than 132,200 Hispanic-
owned businesses operate in the state. Most of California's
Hispanics originated in Mexico, but many recent immigrants
come from El Salvador, Nicaragua, and Guatemala. There are
nearly three million Asian and Pacific Islanders living in
California, more than in any other state. Asians living in
California name China, Japan, the Philippines, and, more recently,
Vietnam and Korea as their country of origin.

POPULATION AND POPULATION DISTRIBUTION

The 1990 census counted 29,760,021 people in California.
California is not only the most populous state in the nation, it
outdistances second-place New York by more than 11 million
people! However, New York City (population 7,322,564) has
3,837,166 more people than second-ranked Los Angeles.

25

Ninety-one of every one hundred residents live in or near a city, making California the nation's second most-urbanized state.

In the Golden State, ninety-one of every one hundred people live in or near a city, making California the nation's second most-urbanized state. California has forty-six cities of 100,000 or more people, most of which lie along the Pacific coastline. California's ten largest cities, in decreasing order, are Los Angeles, San Diego, San Jose, San Francisco, Long Beach, Oakland, Sacramento, Fresno, Santa Ana, and Anaheim.

Much of northern California is wooded and sparsely populated. The San Francisco Bay area, by contrast, teems with more than 5 million people. The southern tip of the bay is the state's fastest growing region. More than 60 percent of Californians live in the third of the state that lies south of the Tehachapi Mountains. In the south, people are concentrated in a narrow strip of land that runs between the Coast Ranges and the Pacific Ocean. Los Angeles, San Diego, and an endless sea of suburbs are packed into this long belt.

In Asian neighborhoods such as San Francisco's Chinatown, Chinese newspapers can be purchased.

LANGUAGES

California's cities, home to great numbers of foreign-born people, are alive with a jumble of languages. In downtown Los Angeles, for example, Spanish is often heard more frequently than English. A corner shop might display a huge sign proclaiming AQUI SE HACEN LLAVES, while below it, a smaller sign reads KEYS MADE HERE. In Asian neighborhoods, an assortment of Chinese, Japanese, Vietnamese, and Korean dialects may be heard.

The diversity of languages spoken in the state became a political issue in 1986. It was proposed that English be the official language of the state, eliminating the need to print documents such as driver's license applications in several languages. Though some Hispanic leaders denounced the idea as racist, a poll conducted by the *Los Angeles Times* determined that 54 percent of the Hispanic citizens favored the proposed law. The proposal was sponsored by S.I. Hayakawa, the state's leading Asian political figure. In the next election, the proposed law passed by a large margin.

LIFE-STYLES

Much of the nation uses images rather than realities when describing how Californians live. The term "laid back" was probably invented in California; it describes a person who is calm and collected, free and easy, "California cool." Of course this image is a myth. Most Californians are hard-working people who hurry through their daily chores with all the speed of New Yorkers. The difference is that Californians get to do everything in pleasant weather.

The car is central to the California life-style. There are almost as many registered motor vehicles in the state as there are people. The tremendous urban sprawl means that anyone who lives in Anaheim but works in Los Angeles spends as much as four hours a day in a car, fighting traffic. California commuters talk about the freeways (highways) the way people elsewhere talk about the weather: "The freeway always clears up by eight at night." "The freeway was a mess yesterday morning."

Californians may well be the most health-and-beauty conscious of all Americans. Joggers pound over sidewalks in nearly every city park. Vegetarian restaurants abound. And only 31 percent of all Californians smoke, far fewer than the national average.

If all Californians were one big family, they would be generally a happy group, but one troubled by frequent and sometimes nasty arguments. Major squabbles occur between northern and southern Californians. Sources of the north vs. south conflicts date back to the 1850s, and concern issues that range from water distribution to political power. But the problems that divide Californians are no greater than those that crop up in other industrial states. The overwhelming majority of residents are proud to call themselves members of the California family.

Chapter 4
THE BEGINNING

THE BEGINNING

My words are one with the great mountains. . .with the great trees.
—A prayer of the Yokut people of old California

THE ORIGINAL CALIFORNIANS

At the time of European contact, between 150,000 and 300,000 people lived in what is today the state of California. The region had the highest concentration of Indians in all of North America. Historians believe the fertile Central Valley was the most densely populated area in the California region.

In old California, the village was the major social unit. Villages were small—even the largest had fewer than a thousand people. Clusters of villages whose people had common bloodlines made up tribes, or ethnic groups. Major groups included the Hupa in the northeast, the Pomo in the region north of San Francisco, the Maidu in central California, the Yuma in the south, and the Mojave in the southeastern desert.

At least twenty-one distinct languages and more than a hundred dialects were spoken in California. A villager who traveled a week's distance from home encountered several people who spoke another language. But despite many linguistic and cultural differences, conflict among villages in California was almost unknown.

For the most part, the original Californians enjoyed a comfortable life in a generous land. In the valleys, the staple food was a paste made from acorn flour. Desert people gathered mesquite beans, and mountain dwellers picked piñon nuts. Inland rivers and lakes teemed with fish that were caught with nets. Skilled hunters brought down deer with arrows, and trappers used ingenious snares to catch rabbits and squirrels. These early Californians practiced conservation and killed only those animals they needed for food. Many tribes uttered ritual prayers, apologizing to the spirit of the animal they killed. They tried to live in harmony with the land.

Original Californians believed in a single creator, as well as a host of lesser gods and spirits. The social and religious center of most villages was the *temescal* (sweat house), a kind of steam bath where men gathered to bathe and to "sweat away" illnesses of the mind or the body. Early Californians wove marvelous baskets from the grasses that grew on their land. Now and then, the people noticed sunlight flashing on bright yellow specks that lay in streambeds. They admired the beauty, but left the metal where it was. The Californians of old had little use or desire for gold.

EXPLORERS AND MISSIONARIES

In the early 1500s, soldiers and explorers from Spain invaded Mexico and South America. The Spaniards were anxious to find gold, and many had read a fabulous story that told of a mythical "island called California" that "abounds with gold and precious stones." Under the spell of this story, the Spaniards gave the name California to the land north of New Spain (Mexico) even before they saw its shores.

In 1542, Juan Rodríguez Cabrillo set sail from Europe, and he became the first European to see the California coastline from the ocean. His ship sailed into San Diego Bay, which he described as "a very good closed port." Cabrillo continued north and passed

In 1579, British adventurer Sir Francis Drake anchored his ship, the *Golden Hind*, somewhere near San Francisco.

San Francisco Bay, apparently without noticing the tremendous gap in the shoreline, now called the Golden Gate and spanned by the Golden Gate Bridge.

About forty years after Cabrillo's voyage, the *Golden Hind*, a ship captained by British adventurer Sir Francis Drake, visited California. Drake's ship anchored somewhere near San Francisco Bay. The exact spot is still in dispute. Drake's chronicler wrote in 1579 that the ship was often surrounded by "stynkinge fogges." Nevertheless, Drake left a brass plate with an engraved message that claimed the land for Queen Elizabeth of England. Great Britain, however, was never able to take control of California. A brass plate meeting the description of the plate Drake left behind was found in 1937 and is currently displayed at the Bancroft Library in Berkeley.

Drake's voyage spurred the Spanish government to launch further explorations of California. In 1584, Francisco Gali discovered Monterey Bay. Sebastián Vizcaíno explored the California coast in 1602 and made a thorough report, urging the king of Spain to colonize the land. But because Spain was committed to developing Mexico, a century and a half passed before a serious effort at the colonization of California began.

Following the orders of Don José de Gálvez, a special deputy of the Spanish king and a man of vision and energy, land and sea parties left what is now Mexico and headed for California. The expedition arrived at San Diego Bay in 1769. Leading the expedition were a Catholic priest, Father Junípero Serra, and a soldier named Gaspar de Portolá. Father Serra and other priests began to build a string of mission churches, starting at San Diego and pushing north along the California coast. Gaspar de Portolá led a party of fifty men on an incredible exploratory march north to San Francisco Bay and back again to San Diego.

The Spaniards who settled in California built forts (*presidios*) and founded agricultural towns (*pueblos*) in the new land. The first two presidios overlooked San Diego and Monterey bays. In 1777, fourteen farming families broke the soil in the Santa Clara Valley; the pueblo they built became the present city of San Jose. Four years later, twelve new families planted crops along the Porciuncula River; their settlement became the sprawling city of Los Angeles. A presidio, a mission, and a pueblo developed almost simultaneously in 1776 when Juan Bautista de Anza led a party of soldiers and settlers to the shores of San Francisco Bay. They called the town they founded *Yerba Buena* (which in English means "good herb") because of the wild vines that grew there. Decades later it was renamed San Francisco.

Most of the soldiers and pioneer farmers who left Mexico to settle in California were *mestizos*. Mestizo is a Spanish word used to describe people of mixed European and Indian bloodlines. The overwhelming majority of modern Mexicans are mestizos. Mestizos today can rightly claim that their ancestors were, after the Indians, the original pioneers of California.

SPANISH CALIFORNIA

Along the California coast, the energetic priest Junípero Serra personally directed the building of nine mission churches. Each mission was a day's journey from the next along a coastal path called *El Camino Real*—the Royal Road.

The Spanish missionaries worked zealously among the Indians who lived near the settlements, trying to persuade them to give up belief in their religion and convert to Christianity. Indians who did convert to Christianity found their lives greatly changed. The Indian converts, called neophytes, were required to live in barracks at the missions. They had to spend many hours a day in prayer, and even more hours tilling the fields or tending the mission's cattle herd. If a neophyte left the mission to return to his people, Spanish soldiers or missionaries conducted a hunt. Once located, the neophyte was forcibly brought back to the mission and punished, often by being tied to the whipping post and lashed.

The normally peaceful California Indians struck back at the missions. Warriors swept out of the hills and burned the missions at San Diego and San Luis Obispo. The Yumas, in particular, were outraged by the invasion of their lands and by the mistreatment they received from the Spanish soldiers and settlers. In 1781, the Yumas destroyed two missions that served as way stations for travelers. Hostility continued into the 1800s, making the overland roads perilous and discouraging new settlement of California from lands to the south.

San Diego de Alcalá was the first Franciscan mission founded by Father Junípero Serra.

The development of agriculture was one of the mission system's most important gifts to early California. Indians who had lived for generations on acorns learned to grow wheat and barley and care for cattle. Mission priests experimented with seeds brought from Spain and Mexico and were the first farmers to plant the fantastic variety of fruits, nuts, and vegetables that thrive in California's soil today.

In 1821, a long and bloody war between Spain and New Spain, her North American colony, ended. New Spain became Mexico, an independent nation. In a bold act, the new government of Mexico stripped California mission churches of their power over the Indians. The neophytes were free—but many had little choice but to take jobs on the Mexican-owned cattle ranches. Worst of all, diseases such as smallpox and measles, formerly confined to Europe, were brought to the New World by whites. These new diseases decimated the Indian population.

During the years of Spanish and later Mexican influence, twenty-one mission churches were built in California. The missions stretched in a chain from San Diego in the south to the Sonoma Valley north of San Francisco Bay. Many of the mission buildings have been restored and, in some cases, totally rebuilt. The missions now stand as popular attractions for tourists and students of California history.

The mission era left California with the legacy of Junípero Serra. In the 1980s, high-ranking members of the Roman Catholic Church proposed to canonize (elevate to sainthood) the dedicated and influential priest. Many Indian leaders oppose the canonization. They claim that Serra, as director of the mission churches, led a system that enslaved Indian peoples. Defenders of Serra concede that abuses took place under the mission system, but argue that Serra himself was innocent of any wrongdoing and always acted as a strenuous defender of Indian rights.

CALIFORNIA UNDER MEXICO

To encourage settlement in California, the Mexican government gave or sold enormous tracts of land to people who agreed to build farms and ranches. In 1839, John Augustus Sutter, an unsuccessful merchant and incurable dreamer, persuaded the Mexican governor to give him a huge parcel of land in the Sacramento Valley. Sutter was once so debt-ridden that he was forced to flee his native Switzerland. But with this generous land grant, he planned to build an agricultural empire—greater than any owned by an Old World monarch. In California, anything was possible.

The Spanish and Mexican settlers (who usually called themselves *Californios*) raised cattle. Nurtured by the thick

Nurtured by the thick grasses, the huge herds of cattle raised by the Californios grew fat and multiplied.

grasses, the animals grew fat and multiplied. A herd of two thousand was considered small. One of the wealthiest of the Californios, Mariano Guadalupe Vallejo, boasted a herd that numbered fifty thousand head of cattle, twenty-four thousand sheep, and eight thousand horses. Other powerful cattle barons included Pio Pico, Jose Figueroa, and Juan Bandini.

Because Indian field hands did nearly all the work, Californios had plenty of free time. Parties at their ranches sometimes lasted a week or more. Guests were served staggering amounts of food and drink and were entertained by guitar-strumming musicians.

Two dark shadows loomed over the Californios' comfortable life-style. First, their numbers were small. At the conclusion of the Mexican War of Independence in 1821, fewer than four thousand non-Indians lived in California. Estimates of the Indian population at that time range from one hundred thousand to two hundred thousand. Second, foreigners—Russians and later Americans—began drifting into the region in increasing numbers.

During the 1840s, hundreds of American settlers made the long and painful trip over deserts and across mountains to California.

MANIFEST DESTINY

During the 1840s, hundreds of American settlers made the long and painful trip over deserts and across mountains to California. The first great wagon train was the Bidwell-Bartleson Party, which arrived in 1841. Another group was the tragic Donner Party, which lost half its members when trapped in the Sierras by a blinding snowstorm.

The American pioneers moved into the western lands with an almost religious belief in America's "manifest destiny." The term meant that American expansion to the Pacific Ocean *must* happen. It made no difference to the American pioneers that Mexico claimed Texas and California, and Britain claimed Oregon.

The manifest destiny fervor was shared by the American military. In 1842, Navy Commander Catesby Jones, acting on the mistaken belief that war had broken out with Mexico, seized Monterey and raised the American flag. When Jones discovered that no war had been declared, he apologized to Mexican officials and sailed away. But the ease with which Jones overtook the garrison at Monterey instilled fear in Mexico City and a sense of confidence among American leaders in Washington, D.C.

The brashest of all Americans to take the field in California was John Charles Frémont. An army officer and the son-in-law of a powerful United States senator, Frémont dreamed of someday running for President. Frémont, and a specially trained unit of sixty men, entered California by crossing the Sierras in 1844. He told Mexican officials he was conducting a peaceful mapmaking survey, but secretly he urged American settlers in California to rebel against Mexican rule.

In 1846, the Bear Flag Revolt broke out when American settlers in northern California raised a banner over the plaza at Sonoma and proclaimed themselves independent from Mexico. The rebels' homemade flag was decorated with a single star and a simply drawn picture of a grizzly bear. A more refined version of that banner now serves as the official state flag of California.

When the Sonoma rebels raised the Bear Flag banner, they did not know that the United States and Mexico were already at war. The immediate causes of the war centered on border disputes in Texas, but in a larger sense, the manifest destiny passion was at the root of the conflict. Only a few skirmishes in the Mexican-American War were actually fought on California soil. More often, California was the scene of outrageous bickering between John Frémont and his fellow officers Steven Watts Kearny and Robert Stockton.

In early 1848, Mexico was defeated and forced to give to the United States a vast expanse of land running from Texas west to the Pacific Ocean. For Americans, the acquisition of the northern Mexican territories meant that the dream of manifest destiny was almost complete. The young American nation now stretched from sea to sea, with only the ownership of the Oregon Territory remaining in doubt. Generations of Mexicans have seethed over the enormity of their loss.

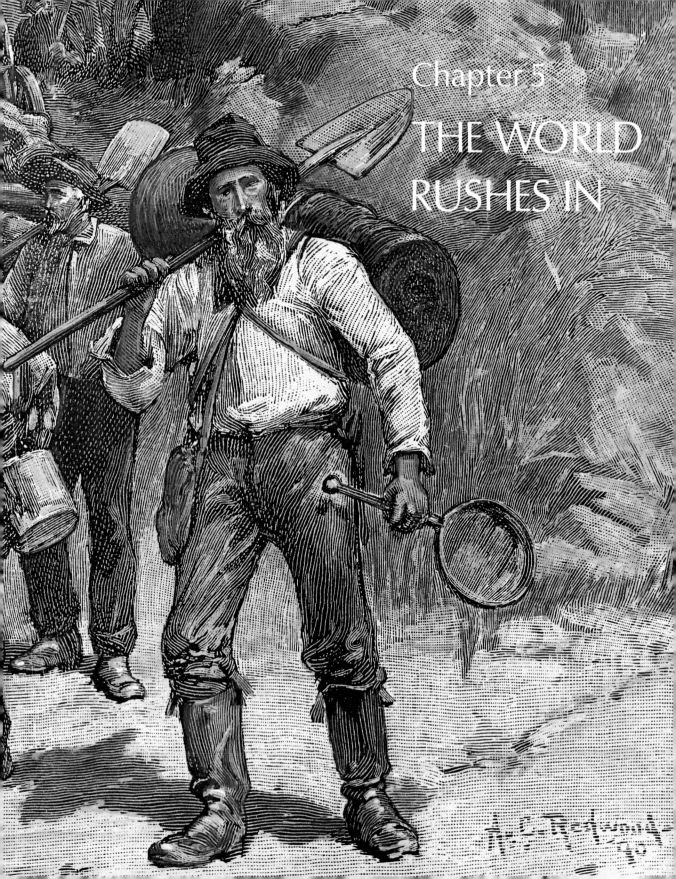

Chapter 5

THE WORLD
RUSHES IN

THE WORLD RUSHES IN

I really hope that no one will be deterred from coming here.
The more fools the better—the fewer to laugh when we get home.
—A letter dated 1850, from the California gold fields

THE DISCOVERY

On a rainy January morning in 1848, John Sutter heard an urgent knock on his door. It was his foreman, James Marshall. Marshall unrolled a cotton cloth containing several nuggets of yellow metal; the largest was about the size of a kernel of unpopped popcorn. Marshall had found the metal pieces in a millrace he was digging along the American River, north and east of what is now Sacramento. Using procedures described in an encyclopedia, Sutter determined that the nuggets were indeed gold. He had no idea those few particles were the seeds of a gold strike so rich that it would change the history of the nation.

Gold fever—an obsessive, insane desire to find and squirrel away the precious yellow metal—soon swept California. The fever spread to the eastern United States, and then to Europe and Asia. Gold fever triggered the great California Gold Rush, the largest and wildest mass movement of people the world had ever seen.

Nothing like the great Gold Rush had happened before 1849, and there has been nothing like it since. At the time James Marshall found the enticing metal sparkling in the streambed, about ten thousand non-Indians lived in California. San Francisco

The discovery of gold at the millrace (left) owned by John Sutter (above) signaled the beginning of the great California gold rush.

was a sleepy village and Sacramento did not exist as a city. Then an army of thousands descended on the region seeking gold and wealth. The bulk of these new arrivals came in that celebrated year, 1849.

THE FORTY-NINERS

In Buffalo, New York, gold fever struck thirty-year-old merchant seaman William Downie, who wrote: "Some of the tales were fabulous, and the reports of treasures found were enough to challenge any man of grit and derring-do. . . . Many, even, who had neither quality, ventured upon the search for gold, prompted merely by the lust for gain. . . ."

Downie was a forty-niner, one of thousands who set out for California in 1849. Most forty-niners were young, unmarried men from middle-class families who had at least a basic education. Few women joined the army of gold-seekers because in 1849, traveling across the continent chasing an adventurer's dream was not considered to be a ladylike activity.

Forty-niners in the gold fields during the California Gold Rush

Forty-niners from the eastern United States could choose one of three routes to get to California. They could travel by sea, travel overland, or travel by a combined land-sea route, which meant crossing the Isthmus of Panama. Each route was filled with hazards, but most forty-niners chose to trek overland on foot or as members of a wagon train. J. L. Stephens, a forty-niner from Marietta, Ohio, survived the rugged hike west. Later he wrote: "The hardships of the overland route to California are beyond conception. Care and suspense, pained anxiety, fear of losing animals . . . fear of being left in the mountains to starve to death, and a thousand other things which no one thinks of until on the way, are things of which I may write and you may read, but they are nothing compared to reality."

Yet they came. By land or sea, ninety thousand gold seekers spilled into California during 1849. Though they suffered tremendous hardships along the way, these were young men who looked upon the journey as an adventure too exciting to miss. When they finally reached California, the forty-niners mustered

44

Storekeepers in the mining areas charged outrageous prices and earned more than the miners earned from gold.

enough energy to sing! Their favorite song—sung to the tune of "Oh, Susannah."—included the following words:

> Oh! California! That's the land for me!
> I'm bound for California with my washbowl on my knee.

LIFE IN THE GOLD FIELDS

Newcomers to the gold fields faced many surprises. First among these were the shocking prices for food and supplies. The mining area had few stores and thousands of customers. Storekeepers earned far more than did the gold miners. A loaf of bread cost $2.00, potatoes were $1.25 a pound, and a pair of boots that went for $2.00 in New York sold for as much as $20.00 in San Francisco. The practice of charging sky-high prices for goods was called "mining the miners."

Early in the Gold Rush days, panning was the common method for extracting gold. To pan, a miner put a small amount of sand and gravel in a pan (kitchen fry pans were often used), dipped the pan into a stream to add a little water, and then swirled the pan carefully. The swirling action washed the dirt away, but the heavier gold remained in the pan. Panning meant a miner had to squat in a cramped position for hours at a time while working with his hands submerged in icy water.

Miners lucky enough to find a new vein of the yellow metal made princely sums—almost overnight. John Sullivan, a former oxcart driver, took $26,000 worth of gold out of a stream he called Sullivan Creek. One miner found $1,500 worth in a single panful of dirt. A boy named Davenport who said he was twelve years old, but looked even younger, found $2,700 worth of gold in only two days.

Fortunes came to some men who never panned or dug for gold. John Studebaker, a carpenter, hammered together wheelbarrows and sold them to miners. Years later, the company he founded became a multimillion-dollar automobile maker. Philip Armour was barely out of his teens when he walked from Stockbridge, New York to California. Believing beef to be more important than gold, he set up a butcher shop that grew into one of the nation's largest food-supply enterprises. Levi Strauss stepped from a ship in San Francisco with dreams of making a pair of pants tough enough to withstand the rigors of a gold miner's working routine. To make his pants stronger, Strauss reinforced the seams with copper rivets. The company he later formed now makes the popular pants the entire world calls Levis.

Most mining camps developed in the lower elevations of the western face of the Sierra Nevadas. That area came to be called Mother Lode Country. The camps were a ragtag collection of tents and log cabins with names such as Git-Up-And-Git, You Bet, Bogus Thunder, and Poker Flat.

In the camps, the young miners grew desperately homesick. Most had dreamed of earning a quick fortune and returning home rich men. But as the months went by, they hungered for their sweethearts and home. Many turned to drinking, reckless gambling, and fighting with other miners.

The great Gold Rush passed John Sutter by. His vast ranch was overrun with gold seekers who trampled his wheat and killed his cattle for food. "The country swarmed with lawless men," Sutter wrote. "Talking with them did no good. I was alone and there was no law." Out of frustration, Sutter tried mining, but found no gold. Ten years after the Gold Rush ended, Sutter was impoverished. And, as a final blow, the United States government refused to recognize the grant from the Mexican government that had given Sutter his vast land holdings. Sutter died alone in a Washington, D.C. hotel, another luckless victim of the Gold Rush.

STATEHOOD

Due to the lure of gold, at the close of 1849 California had enough settlers to apply for statehood. On September 9, 1850, President Millard Fillmore signed the Bill of Admission making California the thirty-first state of the American Union. Peter H. Burnett served as the first governor, and former army captain John C. Frémont was one of its two original United States senators. California leaders squabbled over the location of their capital city, switching it from San Jose, to Vallejo, to Benicia, and, finally, to Sacramento.

Because of California's distance and isolation from Washington, it was nearly two months before the news of its admission to the Union reached San Francisco. When word came, people danced in the streets. The *San Francisco Courier* wrote: "We do not believe that the news of a brilliant victory was ever received by a people with greater joy than was the news yesterday that California is now one of the brightest stars in our glorious galaxy of states."

47

GROWING PAINS

The Gold Rush lasted six short but furious years. By 1855, what miners called "the diggings" were almost exhausted. Certainly gold remained in the hills, but to extract it required engineers, sophisticated equipment, and large crews. Gone were the days when a lone miner could pan a stream and earn a living while dreaming of making a fortune.

The end of the Gold Rush caused a period of financial panic, but the enormous tide of migration to the Golden State continued. From 1850 to 1860, the population of California zoomed from about 100,000 to 379,994. Then, as now, California's population had an international flavor. The 1860 census counted 34,935 Chinese, 33,147 Irish, 21,646 Germans, and a mixture of English, French, Mexicans, Canadians, and Italians. By 1870, one of every four Californians was foreign-born.

Few, if any, cities in the world have experienced the "instant" growth of San Francisco. As was true with most boomtowns, it was not a pretty place. A traveler named Frank Soule wrote: "There was no such thing as a *home* to be found. Scarcely even a proper *house* could be seen. Both dwellings and places of business were either common canvas tents or small rough-born shanties. . . . Only the great gambling saloons, the hotels, restaurants, and a few public buildings had any pretentions to size, comfort, or elegance."

It is estimated that a thousand murders took place in San Francisco during the Gold Rush years of 1849 to 1856. Nearly everyone walking the streets carried some sort of weapon. A particularly bold gang of Australian ex-convicts known as the Sydney Ducks robbed stores even in the middle of the day. The storekeepers organized vigilante committees that rounded up the

Pony Express riders rushed mail from St. Joseph, Missouri to Sacramento in less than ten days. Before the Pony Express, it had taken as long as four months for a letter to arrive from the East.

most troublesome gang members and hung them in Portsmouth Square. At the time, the square was considered to be the city's amusement center.

In 1860, a group of businessmen formed the legendary Pony Express, a mail service that rushed letters from St. Joseph, Missouri, to Sacramento in less than ten days. Before the Pony Express, it took as long as four months for a letter to arrive from the East. The "pony riders," most of whom were teenagers, became heroes in the state. A telegraph line replaced the Pony Express in 1861. Early telegraph messages included news from the fighting fronts of the Civil War, which raged in the eastern states.

The transcontinental railroad, completed in 1869, brought to an end California's isolation from its sister states beyond the mountains to the east. The gleaming silver rail line that ran over mountains and bridged mighty rivers was hailed as an engineering miracle. The railroad was the vision of Theodore

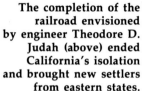

The completion of the railroad envisioned by engineer Theodore D. Judah (above) ended California's isolation and brought new settlers from eastern states.

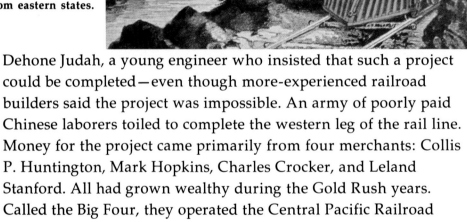

Dehone Judah, a young engineer who insisted that such a project could be completed—even though more-experienced railroad builders said the project was impossible. An army of poorly paid Chinese laborers toiled to complete the western leg of the rail line. Money for the project came primarily from four merchants: Collis P. Huntington, Mark Hopkins, Charles Crocker, and Leland Stanford. All had grown wealthy during the Gold Rush years. Called the Big Four, they operated the Central Pacific Railroad Company of California. The wealth and power of these railroad barons determined the course of the state for decades to come.

The concentration of wealth in just a few hands, combined with overinvesting by state banks in Nevada silver-mining operations, led to a severe economic depression in the 1870s. Many unemployed workers blamed the loss of their jobs on the Chinese. Even after the railroad's completion, Chinese immigrants continued to stream into California. The Chinese were hardworking and willing to accept lower wages than anyone else. In 1871, mobs swept into the Chinese neighborhood in Los

Angeles and lynched at least eighteen innocent people. Six years later, anti-Chinese riots broke out in San Francisco. Throughout the state, anti-Chinese societies were formed.

THE RISE OF THE SOUTH

"Whoever asks where Los Angeles is, to him I shall say: across a desert without wearying, beyond a mountain without climbing . . . in the midst of a garden of thirty-six square miles—there is Los Angeles." Flowery advertising such as this, and a drastic fare war between two railroad companies, induced hordes of people to flock to southern California in the 1880s. Most of the newcomers were eager to buy land. The great migration generated the excitement of a second Gold Rush.

The population of Los Angeles zoomed from six thousand in 1870 to one hundred thousand only thirty years later. In a single year (1885), the price of a small, undeveloped lot in Los Angeles rose from $500 to $5,000 and farmland prices jumped from $350 an acre to $10,000. In the 1890s—spurred by the belief that the year-round warm climate eased the pain of arthritis, asthma, rheumatism, and tuberculosis—people continued to come to southern California. Towns such as Santa Monica, Palm Springs, and Pasadena were developed as health spas. By 1900, one in every ten Californians was a health-seeker hoping to find cures in the sunny climate.

At the turn of the century, California was only fifty years old, yet it was home for almost a million and a half people. Its population had increased almost twenty-fold since statehood. Its farms, its growing factory system, and its powerful banks were the envy of older states. And all over the world, people who yearned for a better life dreamed of California.

Chapter 6
BUILDING THE
CALIFORNIA DREAM

BUILDING THE CALIFORNIA DREAM

*Of all states in the union, only California
has attached to its identity the concept of a dream.*
—Kevin Starr, writer and University of San Francisco professor

THE SAN FRANCISCO EARTHQUAKE

At five in the morning, April 18, 1906, policeman Jesse Cook walked his beat on the streets of San Francisco. He noticed horses snorting nervously in their stalls and backyard dogs locked in an eerie chorus of howls. Officer Cook had no idea that animals are strangely attuned to the urgent grindings that take place deep inside the earth, the grindings that foretell the coming of an earthquake. Then, for no apparent reason, the bell at old St. Mary's Church began to toll crazily. "There was a deep rumble, deep and terrible," Cook said. "And then I could see it actually coming up Washington Street. The whole street was undulating. It was as if the waves of the ocean were coming toward me."

The first tremor rattled the city for forty seconds. Next came ten seconds of absolute stillness. Then, a second tremor started and rumbled for twenty seconds.

In all, the great San Francisco Earthquake lasted less than a minute and a half, but it left a smashed and dazed city. Tiny row houses were wrenched about so their front windows now faced their neighbors' lots. Brick walls on downtown buildings collapsed, leaving only the steel superstructures standing.

During the 1906 San Francisco earthquake, buildings toppled and fires raged, sending people to safety outside the city.

At least fifty small fires broke out minutes after the quake. The city's superb fire department was unable to fight the blazes because the earthquake had broken the underground water pipes. Fire hydrants were useless. By afternoon, the winds whipping off the waterfront swirled the small fires into one raging sheet of flame.

As night fell, the roads became choked with people marching slowly out of the doomed city. Remarkably, there was little panic. Bertha Nienberg, a small girl clinging to her mother's hand, later wrote: "There was no sign of tears. No moans, no shrieks, no hysteria. It was a dignified procession."

The fire raged unchecked for three days. At least seven hundred people died in the twin disasters. The fire caused far more casualties than the earthquake. Some three hundred thousand people lost their homes, and property damage exceeded $500 million. But within ten years, a new and far more beautiful city rose from the ashes of the old.

The swelling population in the early twentieth century led to the growth of industry and agriculture. The oil industry flourished and fruit brought more money to the state than any other product.

INDUSTRY AND REFORM

On the afternoon of the San Francisco Earthquake, flames threatened the tiny Bank of Italy building. The bank's owner, Amadeo Peter Giannini, borrowed a horse and wagon and loaded it with his most valuable records and a sackful of cash. When he was safely away from the flames, Giannini hammered together a crude plank counter and immediately went to work lending money so that people could rebuild their homes. When Giannini died in 1949, his institution, renamed the Bank of America, was the world's largest bank and held assets worth $8.2 billion.

Banking was only one of many businesses that blossomed in the early twentieth century. An oil field at Long Beach's Signal Hill proved to be among the richest of such fields in the world. Fruit, shipped to the east by railroad refrigerator cars, brought more money to California than any other product. And the most glamorous business of all, the motion-picture industry, grew in the Los Angeles neighborhood called Hollywood.

Railroad companies held more cash and owned more property than any other business. Their owners wielded power over politicians, and the state legislature passed many laws that were favorable to the railroads. In 1910, fiery lawyer Hiram Johnson ran for governor on the platform "Get the Southern Pacific Railroad Company out of politics!" Johnson was elected in 1910 and re-elected in 1914. Under his leadership, the legislature passed a series of reforms that included the following: the creation of a commission to regulate railroad freight rates, a law to compensate workers injured on the job, a law prohibiting child labor in California, and a bill allowing women to vote.

Industrial expansion during and immediately after World War I brought a fresh wave of immigrants, most of whom settled in the south. In 1920, the population of Los Angeles reached more than a half million and, for the first time since California achieved statehood, surpassed the population of San Francisco. An efficient network of electric streetcars carried people to and from Los Angeles' sprawling neighborhoods in far better time than today's traffic-clogged freeways.

Hollywood became California's silver window to the world during the 1920s. In those days, movies had no sound, and they were shown on screens that were tiny compared to today's modern screens. Yet to millions of people around the world, *Hollywood* and *movies* were almost the same word.

HARD TIMES

The Great Depression of the 1930s shut down California's buzzing factories and shipyards. By 1934, one in five California workers was unemployed and collecting some form of assistance. California's depression problems deepened when a terrible

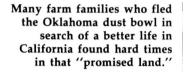
Many farm families who fled the Oklahoma dust bowl in search of a better life in California found hard times in that "promised land."

drought hit Oklahoma and parts of Texas, creating what was called a "dust bowl." Farm families loaded their possessions into cars and trucks and drove west. They hoped to find jobs picking fruit in California. Instead, they faced hostility from the Californians, many of whom were themselves seeking work desperately. The plight of the dust-bowl migrants was powerfully described in John Steinbeck's novel *The Grapes of Wrath*. Today, much of the Central Valley from Bakersfield to Sacramento is populated by the people who came to California during the grim Dust Bowl era.

Leading a movement called EPIC (End Poverty in California), writer Upton Sinclair ran for governor in 1934. He proposed to tax the wealthy in order to create jobs for the poor. Opponents denounced Sinclair as a Communist, an infidel, and worse. In the election, Sinclair received almost a million votes, narrowly losing to the Republican candidate, Frank F. Merriam.

CALIFORNIA AT WAR

The Japanese bombs that blasted Pearl Harbor on December 7, 1941, shocked all Americans, but Californians felt a special concern. California, of course, is the state closest to Hawaii. Residents worried that San Francisco, Los Angeles, or San Diego might be bombed next. People openly wondered if the Japanese would invade the California coast.

In their fear, Californians and other West Coast residents spread vicious rumors about Japanese Americans. People claimed to have heard Japanese Americans talking to Tokyo on secret radios. Some said that Japanese farmers plowed their fields in the shape of arrows to direct bombers toward factory buildings and key bridges. Not a shred of evidence existed that any Japanese person—United States citizen or resident alien—committed a single act of spying or sabotage. Nevertheless, the hysteria led to a demand that all residents of Japanese ancestry be forcibly moved away from the West Coast states.

In February 1942, two months after Pearl Harbor, President Franklin D. Roosevelt signed Executive Order 9066—all people of Japanese ancestry were to be moved away from California, Oregon, and Washington. The people were herded into barbed-wire-enclosed compounds at dusty mountain sites. There they spent the remainder of the war years under guard. In spite of this outrageous treatment, Japanese American soldiers, many from California, became members of the 442nd Regiment. During the war in Europe, soldiers of the 442 won more medals for bravery than those of any other World War II unit.

As the war raged, California served as a vital arsenal for the nation. In 1944 alone, the aviation industry produced nearly one hundred thousand planes. Shipyards in Eureka, Humboldt Bay,

San Francisco, Vallejo, Richmond, Oakland, Alameda, San Pedro, and Los Angeles worked around the clock. The huge Kaiser Shipyards at Richmond employed one hundred thousand workers. Shipyard crews once assembled an entire freight-hauling Liberty ship in only eight days.

For the first time in the state's history, large numbers of black people migrated to California. One of every four blacks who left the South during the war years moved to the Golden State. From 1940 to 1945, the state's black population doubled. Blacks continued to come from the South long after the war ended. Drawn by industrial jobs, most of them settled in the state's urban areas.

In April 1945, even while the war was being fought, delegates from fifty countries met in San Francisco to organize the United Nations. Around the world, people weary of war looked to San Francisco in the hope that the newly formed United Nations could provide a lasting peace.

POSTWAR PROSPERITY

When the war finally ended, thousands of transplanted war workers and military personnel decided to settle permanently in the Golden State. Through great foresight, California was prepared to provide needed services for these newcomers. Governor Earl Warren, who served from 1943 to 1953, had kept taxes high during the war years, thereby creating a "rainy day fund." This meant that there was money available to build schools and roadways to serve the ever-expanding population.

During the decade of the 1950s, 3.1 million people relocated to California. In 1963, the population surpassed that of New York, and California became the nation's most-populous state.

A fanciful picture of California was sent to the world through a series of lively beach-party movies that were popular in the late 1950s and early 1960s. The movies portrayed Californians as young, perfectly built, beautiful people who never worried about money and had little else to do but frolic on the beach. The beach-party movies gave the impression that the California dream had become a reality, but these movies failed to show a grimmer side of California life.

THE TURBULENT YEARS

"I can't get a job and I've been trying . . . when I take in an application they say, 'Well, we'll call you, we'll call you,' but you never get any action." These were the words of Marquette Frye, a Watts resident whose arrest for drunken driving triggered the great Los Angeles race riots of 1965.

In the mid-1960s, the Los Angeles community of Watts did not resemble the slums of the older, eastern cities. On the contrary, its streets were broad, and most of its residents lived in one- and two-story frame and stucco homes. Watts was located in the midst of California's affluence, but its people felt they were on the outside looking in. Almost all the residents of Watts were black; most were recent migrants from the South. Unemployment in the black community had skyrocketed, and the school dropout rate was double the city's average. Watts residents looked upon the nearly all-white Los Angeles Police Department as if it were an enemy army occupying their homeland. A black judge noted that "the people distrust the police and the police distrust the people. They move in a constant atmosphere of hate."

On a broiling summer night in 1965, a crowd gathered while police made a routine traffic arrest. Someone threw a rock, more

During the 1965 Watts riot, the streets looked like a combat zone in wartime.

police arrived, a gunshot pierced the night, and Watts exploded
into one of the worst race riots in American history. For four
nights, mobs looted stores, burned cars, and exchanged gunfire
with the police. Some police compared the streets of Watts to a
combat zone in wartime. When calm was finally restored, thirty-
four people were dead, more than a thousand people were
injured, and property damage topped $40 million.

The late 1960s and early 1970s were angry years in California
and in the nation. Violence flared up during the long and bitter
Delano Grape Strike organized by Cesar Chavez. A "Free Speech
Movement" began at the University of California's Berkeley
campus and led to clashes between students and campus police.
The frustrating and prolonged Vietnam War prompted students to
demonstrate against the university's Reserve Officers Training
Corps (ROTC) program.

Los Angeles sparkles on breezy days (left), but smog hangs over the city when there is no wind to clear out the air pollution from automobiles and factories.

Pledging to end campus disturbances, former Hollywood star Ronald Reagan ran for governor in 1966. He beat incumbent Pat Brown handily, but campus riots continued at Berkeley and spread to other schools in the University of California system. For many Americans, the unrest at Berkeley symbolized the student violence that shook the rest of the nation in the 1960s.

Aside from the violence of the era, the 1960s also bred a new awareness in people. Californians saw with horror the effects of automobile and industrial pollution. On breezeless days, the emissions from millions of cars hung over Los Angeles in a soupy, yellowish cloud. Los Angeles residents demanded that their government require manufacturers to install pollution-control devices on autos. But few residents would go so far as to urge government leaders to build subways and improve train service to decrease Californians' dependence on automobiles. In San Francisco and Santa Monica, however, the people joined a "freeway revolt" and blocked efforts to build new highways through their cities.

ISSUES OF THE EIGHTIES

In 1980, former governor Ronald Reagan was elected president of the United States, the second Californian to serve in that office. Several writers pointed out that Reagan was more-typically Californian than Richard Nixon. Though Nixon had been born in the state, Reagan, like the majority of Californians, had been born elsewhere.

In 1981, swarms of Mediterranean fruit flies descended on California. Farm groups wanted to spray the insects immediately, before they destroyed valuable crops. Conservationists opposed spraying because they feared the chemicals would harm the environment. Governor Jerry Brown—son of Pat Brown, California governor during the 1960s—wavered between the two positions before finally deciding to allow the spraying to take place from helicopters and airplanes. His weeks of indecision irritated the voters.

Tom Bradley, the mayor of Los Angeles, came within a few thousand votes of being elected the state's first black governor in 1982. Four years later, Bradley lost the governorship by a larger margin. Meanwhile, black political leader Willie Brown, Speaker of the State Assembly, rose to great power in the 1980s.

The color and drama of the Olympic Games once again came to Los Angeles in 1984. The city had first hosted the games in 1932. The huge Los Angeles Coliseum served as the main arena for both events. The extravagantly staged 1984 Games were marred because the Soviet Union and most Eastern European countries boycotted them for political reasons.

Disgust with ever-rising street crime moved voters during 1986. Rose Bird, the first woman ever to serve as chief justice of the California Supreme Court, was voted out of office largely because

The Los Angeles Coliseum
served as the main arena for
the 1984 summer Olympic Games.

Californians believed she coddled criminals. Governor George
Deukmejian's tough stance on crime was a major factor in his
successful bid for a second term. Voters in the charming city of
Carmel-by-the-Sea chose movie actor Clint Eastwood to be their
mayor. Eastwood may have influenced a few voters through his
role as a courageous and forceful cop in the "Dirty Harry" series
of movies.

Great numbers of people from Latin America and Asia settled in
California during the 1980s. A 1965 change in immigration laws
allowed thousands of Asians to come to the United States, and
many decided to make California their home. The Mexican
economy suffered a collapse in the 1980s, and a crush of desperate
workers came to the United States looking for jobs. Although
most Mexicans and Latin Americans had proper immigration
papers, there are estimates that 1.5 to 3 million people crossed the
American border illegally. At least half of those illegal aliens live
and work in California.

From every point in the world, people continue to rush to
California, seeking their share of the California dream.

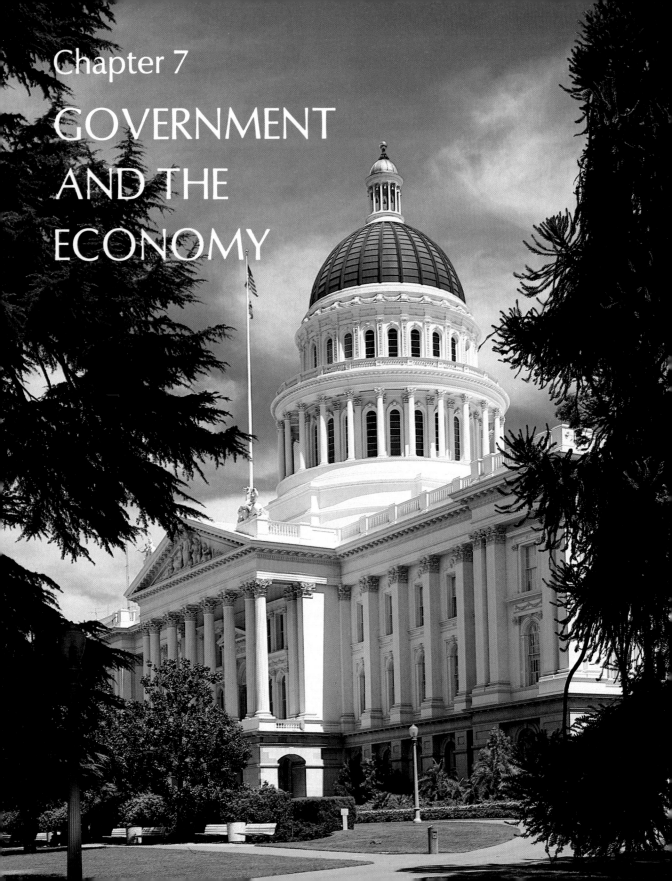

Chapter 7

GOVERNMENT AND THE ECONOMY

GOVERNMENT AND THE ECONOMY

California's factories and fields are first in the nation in the production of food and manufactured goods. Its government is a huge, complex organization that employs thousands of men and women.

THE GOVERNMENT OF CALIFORNIA

The current state constitution, adopted in 1879 and amended more than 350 times since, separates the government into three branches: executive, legislative, and judicial. In theory, each branch acts as a check on the others' power.

The executive branch is charged with carrying out laws. It is headed by the governor, whose powers and responsibilities include pardoning people in prison and calling out the state militia in times of emergency. The governor can also veto, or reject, a proposed law sent to him by the state legislature. Other important officers in the executive branch are the lieutenant governor, the secretary of state, the attorney general, the treasurer, and the superintendent of public instruction. All of these officers are elected to four-year terms.

The California legislature consists of a forty-member senate and an eighty-member assembly. Men and women who sit in the legislature propose laws, called bills. Once a majority of legislators agrees on the details of a bill, it is sent to the governor. When signed by the governor, the bill becomes a law. If the governor vetos a bill, the legislature can, with a two-thirds majority vote, override the veto. In such a case, the bill becomes law regardless of the governor's wishes.

The judicial department interprets laws and hears evidence and testimony when a person is accused of a crime. The highest judicial body is the state supreme court, composed of a chief justice and six associate justices. If the state supreme court determines that a law violates the state constitution, the court can strike down that law, even though it was passed by a majority of the legislature and signed by the governor.

The state constitution allows citizens to take the initiative and pass laws directly. If 5 percent of the voters sign a petition favoring a proposed law, then this proposition will appear on the ballot in the next general election. If approved by a majority of the voters, the proposition will become a law. In this manner, Proposition 13 restricted the amount of tax the government could exact from property owners, and Proposition 63 made English the official language of the state.

California's 58 counties, 438 cities, and more than 1,000 school districts make up its local government complex. Local services such as staffing libraries and maintaining police forces require both workers and money. In 1987, for example, the state employed 1,205,600 local government workers.

EDUCATION

Public schools consume more than half the state's annual budget. State law requires students to attend school from age six through age eighteen. However, any student over the age of fifteen who graduates or passes a qualifying examination may

Stanford University in Palo
Alto (left) and the University
of Southern California in Los
Angeles (above) are among the
state's private universities.

leave school or seek to enter a community college. In spite of this
law, 18 percent of California's students fail to complete high
school; the national average is 12 percent. Dropouts face a difficult
future because without at least a high-school education, it is
nearly impossible to find a decent job in California's highly
technical economy.

One of every eight primary and secondary pupils attends a
private school. Most private schools are church-affiliated, with the
Roman Catholic Church school system being the largest. While
the private school system is growing, public schools remain the
norm in California. Pride in public schools is a California
tradition.

For many years, California has had fine public and private
universities. Between 1923 and 1986, California college professors
won forty Nobel Prizes. The University of California's Berkeley
campus leads the list with thirteen Nobel Prize winners, while
Stanford professors have won ten of the prestigious awards.
Berkeley and Stanford are among the finest centers of higher
learning in the nation. Many other California universities have
also won academic honors.

California's computer and computer-related industries are concentrated in Silicon Valley, a fast-growing area between San Jose and Palo Alto.

PRODUCTS OF THE FACTORIES

More than two million Californians hold factory jobs. Aircraft factories are centered in the south, where pilots can test planes in virtually cloudless skies. Automobiles are assembled in Alameda County and in plants scattered throughout Los Angeles and Santa Clara counties. About two thousand California plants produce electrical machinery ranging from gigantic hydroelectric generators to household-size automatic can openers. Other plants build construction equipment and office machines. Printing, textiles, and wood products are important to the economy. Steel mills operate in Fontana, Torrance, Los Angeles, San Francisco and a town appropriately named for steel production—Pittsburg, California.

One in every five workers is employed in the high-tech aerospace or computer fields. Computer-related industries in "Silicon Valley" near San Jose employ 231,000 people.

California has the dubious honor of producing more devices designed to kill than any other state in the Union. The MX missile, the Tomahawk cruise missile, the B-1 and the Stealth bombers, as well as the latest and swiftest fighter planes for the air force and the navy, are designed and produced in California. The state's factories turned out $28 billion worth of weapons in 1984 alone. In 1987, California's aerospace firms won most of the contracts awarded to build the highly controversial SDI, or "Star Wars," missile-defense system. Few states other than California have the engineers and skilled workers necessary to produce these complex weapons systems.

The food-processing industry is the outgrowth of the state's large, rich farms. California leads the nation in canning, freezing, and drying foods. About 90 percent of the wine made in the United States comes from California wineries.

PRODUCTS OF THE FIELDS

Most farms in the Golden State are large and specialized, and employ highly technical machines. The tendency toward large farms started a century ago, and today corporate-owned, rather than family-owned, farms are the norm. Many areas are especially suited to growing a particular crop. For example, the majority of fields in the Napa Valley produce only grapes for the wine industry. Farms near the town of Gilroy grow garlic almost exclusively. The pungent smell can be detected miles away.

Superb soil, plenty of sunny days, irrigation, and modern techniques account for California's bountiful yields. Fewer than 1 percent of the state's people work the soil, and only a tiny portion of its land is devoted to farming, yet California has led all other states in total farm production for more than forty years.

Half the fresh fruits, nuts, and vegetables that Americans buy in stores are grown in the Golden State. California is America's number one producer of tomatoes for processing, olives, onions, potatoes, asparagus, avocados, broccoli, carrots, celery, lettuce, apricots, grapes, melons, almonds, walnuts, peaches, pears, and plums. Only Florida leads California in the production of oranges.

About 3.5 million beef cattle graze on California ranches. Dairy farmers milk 1.1 million cows. Poultry producers deliver $372 million worth of eggs each year, leading the nation in that department.

California farmers and ranchers are assisted in their work by agricultural research conducted in the state's universities. The University of California's Davis and Riverside campuses have advanced agricultural programs, as do the California State Universities at Fresno and at Chico.

IRRIGATION SYSTEMS

California's miraculous agricultural production and its growth as a state were made possible through the ability of engineers to move water from one place to another. Almost 40 percent of the state's water reserves lie in the northwest, where only 2 percent of the people live. Had it not been for the construction of irrigation systems, much of southern California would be geographically identified as a desert or a semi-desert. Though the need for transporting water seems obvious, water projects have had a stormy history.

In the early 1900s, William Mulholland, a one-time ditch digger who worked his way up to head the Los Angeles Water Department, looked north to the Owens River Valley for the water supply Los Angeles would need if it were to grow. Under

Thanks to irrigation, Napa Valley vineyards produce bountiful harvests for the California wine industry.

Mulholland's direction, the complex and costly Los Angeles Aqueduct was built. But the aqueduct robbed water from four thousand Owens Valley farmers. The outraged farmers sued in court and a few even dynamited dams along the aqueduct system. Despite their protests, the aqueduct's operations continued.

Development in the Imperial Valley was set back in the early 1900s when floodwaters from the Colorado River wiped out farms and villages and created what is now the Salton Sea. The Colorado River was finally controlled with the completion of the Hoover Dam in 1936. The All American Canal, a concrete-lined irrigation channel, now brings water from the Colorado River to the Imperial Valley. Enjoying a three-hundred-day growing season, each acre in the valley produces a ton of cotton a year.

In 1951, the Central Valley Project began operations. It channeled water away from the Sacramento Valley and into the San Joaquin Valley. Another system called the California Water Project also shifted water from north to south. This reassignment

Shasta Dam, on the Sacramento River, is one of the many dams that was built as part of the vast California water projects.

In modern California, logging is a carefully controlled industry, in sharp contrast to the wasteful methods employed in the past.

of water reserves is one of the issues that divides northern and southern California into separate, and sometimes hostile, camps. In 1982, voters rejected a proposed Central Valley canal project. It was the first time ever that Californians voted against a major water project.

The vast California water projects necessitated the building of many dams. Often these dams were constructed under difficult conditions, and they now stand as monuments to the state's engineering genius. One of the earliest structures is the Shasta Dam, which created Lake Shasta on the Sacramento River. Shasta is also one of the world's highest dams. The Imperial Dam, the Folsom Dam, the Friant Dam, and the Oroville Dam are other engineering marvels that help regulate the flow of water in the Golden State.

MINES, MINERALS, FORESTRY, FISHING

Almost a century and a half after James Marshall's startling gold find, the precious metal is still being mined in California.

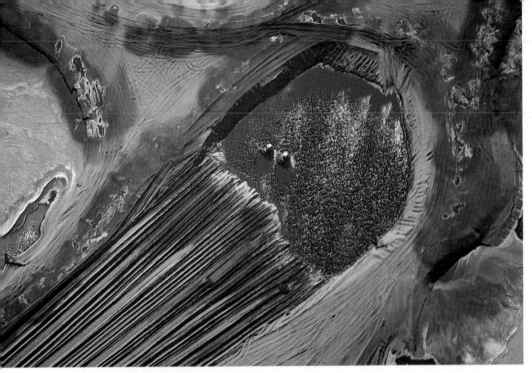

California's oil production ranks fourth in the nation. Petroleum coke, shown here in an aerial view at the Concord Oil Refinery, is a by-product of the crude-oil refining process.

Today's gold output totals about $16 million each year. Silver, tungsten, copper, zinc, mercury, gypsum, and sand and gravel are all taken from California's mineral-rich soil. The state is the nation's only producer of boron—a mineral kept in everyone's pantry in the form of kitchen cleanser.

The state's oil industry began in 1892, when enterprising lawyer Edward Doheny suspected that the ground under a Los Angeles neighborhood might yield what is often called black gold. Drilling spread out to the southern San Joaquin Valley and the coast near Long Beach. Today, California has 47,000 working oil wells. Its oil production ranks fourth in the nation and its production of natural gas ranks seventh.

California trails only Oregon and Washington in the production of forest products. Commercial forestland is concentrated in the north. In modern California, logging is a carefully controlled industry, in sharp contrast to the wasteful methods employed in the past. Most of the state's lumber companies are obliged to plant trees to replace those they cut down.

Commercial fishing boats moored in San Diego Harbor

Day in and day out, sixteen thousand California fishermen venture out in more than five thousand boats to bring in the catch. Tuna, followed by halibut and herring, are the most important fish taken from California's coastal waters. More than seven thousand people work in the state's fish-processing plants.

TRANSPORTATION AND COMMUNICATION

California's first freeway, opened in 1940, linked Los Angeles with Pasadena. It was a harbinger of today's incredible network of roads and highways. However, the state also has 14 million registered cars, 3.9 million trucks, 1.7 million trailers, and 700,000 motorcycles. This swarm of vehicles often turns one of the world's largest highway systems into a snarling traffic jam.

In the early 1960s, the people of the San Francisco Bay area elected to invest in mass transit rather than build more freeways. Thus, the Bay Area Rapid Transit (BART) was born. This ultramodern subway system rushes people from San Francisco to Oakland and the surrounding communities. After a decade of expanding their highway system, Los Angeles has finally decided to invest in mass transit in order to alleviate traffic problems. In 1986, ground was broken for a subway system that will carry more than three hundred thousand people a day when it is completed in 1992.

Scores of mighty bridges span channels in the Golden State. The most-famous bridges have been erected in the San Francisco Bay area, and include the San Francisco-Oakland Bay Bridge, the Richmond-San Rafael Bridge, and the queen of them all—the Golden Gate Bridge.

California's busiest airports are at Los Angeles and San Francisco. Each year, more oceangoing vessels call at the Port of Los Angeles than at any other United States port. Oakland is the state's second-busiest port city. San Diego is the home port for the United States Pacific Fleet, the world's mightiest flotilla. Oceangoing ships push through a deep channel as far inland as Sacramento and Stockton. Although the state's railroads haul thousands of tons of freight, passenger service is now limited to the major cities.

The three largest daily newspapers are the *Los Angeles Times*, the *San Francisco Chronicle*, and the *Orange County Register*. More than forty-six thousand people work in California's newspaper business. The most glamorous communication enterprise—the motion-picture industry—is no longer concentrated in Hollywood. But studios there produce many television programs and made-for-TV movies.

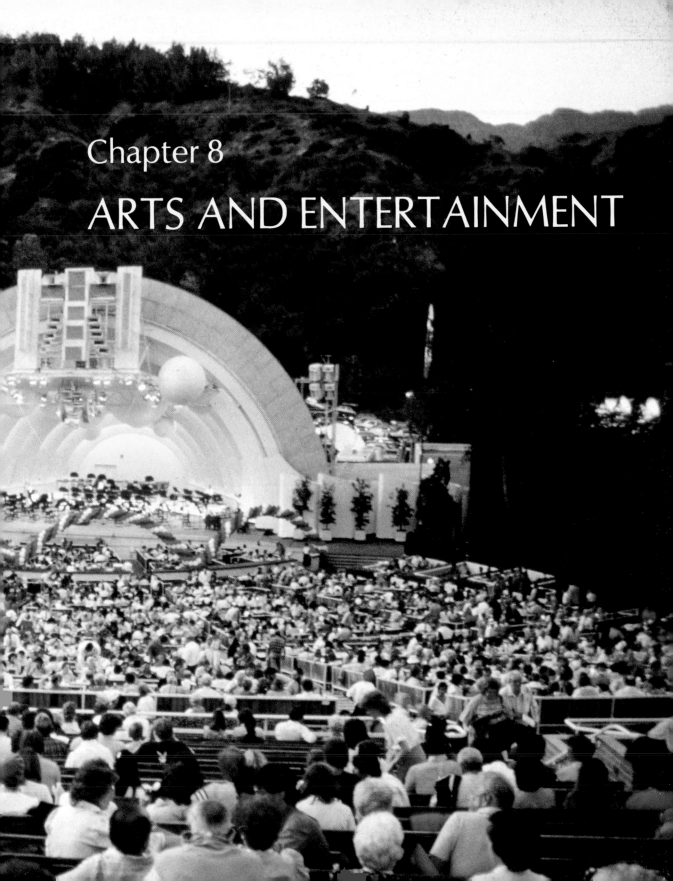

Chapter 8
ARTS AND ENTERTAINMENT

ARTS AND ENTERTAINMENT

Hard work made California an industrial and agricultural giant, but its citizens are famous for their love of fun. During their leisure hours, Californians pursue pleasure and the arts with zeal.

LITERATURE

California's literary tradition goes back to the 1850s, when Bret Harte wrote short stories with Gold Rush settings. "The Luck of Roaring Camp" told how an orphaned baby changed the lives of a group of down-and-outers in a gold-mining village. Harte also wrote other Gold Rush stories, including "The Outcasts of Poker Flat." Harte's friend Samuel Clemens, better known as Mark Twain, wrote the lively satirical story "The Celebrated Jumping Frog of Calaveras County." Twain journeyed the world and described the trip in fifty letters published in the San Francisco paper *Alta California*. The letters were later published in his book *Innocents Abroad*, one of the author's most popular works.

Ambrose Bierce commanded California's literary scene in the late 1800s. As a youth, Bierce fought in the Civil War, and the memory of bloody battlefields haunted him the rest of his life. An eerie theme of death is present in nearly all of Bierce's stories. As an old man, Bierce traveled to Mexico, where he mysteriously disappeared.

Frank Norris wrote an influential novel called *The Octopus*

John Steinbeck (above), author of such novels as *Cannery Row, Tortilla Flat*, and *The Grapes of Wrath*, grew up in this house in Salinas.

(1901), which described the ties between millionaire railroad owners and corrupt California politicians. At about the same time, poet George Sterling founded a writers' colony at the town of Carmel-by-the-Sea, more commonly referred to as Carmel. Members of the colony included novelist Mary Austin and poet Ina Coolbrith. Upton Sinclair, Sinclair Lewis, and San Francisco-born Jack London were frequent visitors to the Carmel group. Many of London's books and short stories were raw, action-filled tales based on his experiences as a sailor on the high seas and as a prospector in the Alaskan gold fields.

John Steinbeck set most of his books in California. Born in Salinas, Steinbeck wrote novels such as *Cannery Row* and *Tortilla Flat*, whose principle characters were poor farmers and workers. His most famous novel, *The Grapes of Wrath*, focused on a struggling family of farm workers trying to find a better life in California during the depression-rocked 1930s.

One of America's greatest playwrights was William Saroyan, who was born in Fresno and set many of his plays in that city. As a child, Saroyan once attempted to read every book in the Fresno Public Library. Many of his characters were poor but dignified working men and women. Saroyan's most famous play, *The Time of Your Life*, examines the lives of a group of people who frequent a waterfront saloon.

A literary revolution took place during the 1950s when poet Lawrence Ferlinghetti opened his City Lights Bookshop in San Francisco. The store became a gathering place for young poets, novelists, playwrights, and others. Jack Kerouac, a famous 1950s novelist, said the City Lights crowd felt "a weariness with all the forms, all the conventions of the world. . . . So I guess you might say we're a beat generation." Thus, San Francisco became the headquarters for the "beat writers" and their followers, who were called beatniks.

Some modern California writers enjoy taking jabs at the institutions of their state. Science-fiction writer Ray Bradbury chided Californians for their dependence on the automobile in "The Last Pedestrian." Novelist Joan Didion's book *Play It As It Lays* describes the loose life-style of southern California pleasure seekers.

THE FINE ARTS

California's earliest art was in the form of superb rock paintings drawn by Indian artists more than a thousand years ago. Spanish priests marveled at the Indians' talent in painting, sculpture, and weaving. Many of the magnificent paintings and wood carvings that adorn the walls of the original twenty-one missions were created by Indian neophytes.

The ornate design of the towers built in Watts by Italian folk artist Simon Rodia (left) stands in sharp contrast to the clean lines of this Isamu Noguchi sculpture in Costa Mesa (above).

Probably the finest Gold Rush artist was German-born Charles Nahl, whose best-known paintings are *Sunday Morning in the Mines* and *Fandango*. Albert Bierstadt, also born in Germany, painted striking pictures of the high Sierras and the Yosemite Valley.

Two California photographers, Ansel Adams and Edward Weston, elevated photography to a fine-art form. Both men ascribed to the school called straight photography, which sought to achieve dramatic results through simple and direct pictures. In one of the most haunting photographs ever taken, Adams captured the afternoon moon rising over the Yosemite Valley. Many of Edward Weston's photos concentrated on the wonderful forms and rolling seas of sand in the Mojave Desert.

Though nearly all California cities are graced with sculptures, one of the most unusual examples is Watts Towers in the Watts neighborhood of Los Angeles. The sculpture is the work of an Italian immigrant named Simon Rodia, who began to build it in his backyard after he returned from the trenches of World War I. The work consists of three lacy spires and four smaller towers, all made of reinforced concrete and adorned with tilings.

Among California's many architectural treasures are San Diego de Alcalá, the first mission built by Father Junípero Serra, and the Transamerica Pyramid, designed by architect William Pereira and built in 1972 in downtown San Francisco.

Sculptor Isamu Noguchi designed the California Scenario, a magnificent sculpture garden that completely surrounds the Orange County Performing Arts Center in Costa Mesa.

California boasts many architectural masterpieces. The state's twenty-one missions are perhaps its most treasured structures. The Carmel Mission is the most famous, but many lovers of architecture prefer the graceful Spanish-Moorish look of Mission San Gabriel Archángel in San Gabriel. The First Church of Christ, Scientist at Berkeley charms the viewer with its flowing lines. The Hollyhock House, built in 1910 in Los Angeles by architect Frank Lloyd Wright, features canted walls, adorned with rich decorations. Excellent examples of modern architecture include the Fulton Street Mall in Fresno, the Transamerica Pyramid in San Francisco, and the Crystal Palace in Garden City.

PERFORMING ARTS

In the Gold Rush era, miners willingly paid a week's earnings to see a song-and-dance performer on stage. Since they were almost entirely cut off from the company of women, they paid double if the entertainment were provided by a female performer. Lola Montez, a dancer with a colorful past, took advantage of this unique opportunity. She earned a small fortune by dancing and singing for the miners—even though she was a terrible dancer and an even worse singer. Finally, perhaps mercifully, Lola Montez retired from the stage to devote her attention to teaching. Her prize pupil was a bright-eyed nine-year-old bundle of talent named Lotta Crabtree. Little Lotta reminded homesick miners of their younger sister or their favorite niece. Wherever she sang and danced, a grateful audience showered her with coins and bags of gold dust.

Chinese theater was popular in San Francisco in the 1850s and thrived for more than a hundred years. The plays were the retellings of classic Chinese folktales. Acts could last as long as five hours, and the spectators ate and gossiped during much of the performance—but as soon as an important passage began, the theater became respectfully silent.

Since those early days, California has become a center for the performing arts. The state has forty-nine major symphony orchestras, seventeen opera companies, eighteen classical choral groups, four professional ballet companies, and more than two hundred major dance organizations.

San Francisco, which has a symphony orchestra, an opera company, and a ballet company, is also home to several theater and dance companies. The American Conservatory Theatre is the largest resident theater company in the nation. Two of the most prestigious dance companies are Theater Flamenco, a Spanish dance company, and the Margaret Jenkins Dance Company, a modern and experimental dance group.

The Los Angeles Music Center is one of the two major settings for classical music in Los Angeles. The other is the Hollywood Bowl, one of the world's largest natural amphitheaters.

The San Diego Repertory Theater holds an annual Shakespeare festival at the Old Globe Theater, a replica of the original Shakespeare theater at Stratford-on-Avon. Elizabethan music and drama, as well as an annual Shakespeare festival are presented at Carmel's Forest Theatre.

Among the many musical events that take place every year in California, five are especially noteworthy: the Monterey Jazz Festival, the Carmel Bach Festival, the Cabrillo Music Festival in Santa Cruz, the Mozart Festival in San Luis Obispo, and the Sacramento Dixieland Jazz Festival.

THE MOVIES

An old song begins with the words "Hooray for Hollywood! That screwy, ballyhooey Hollywood . . . ." The song lauds the town that was for decades California's window to miracles.

Hollywood became the movie capital of the world when director D. W. Griffith created his masterpieces, *The Birth of a Nation* (1915) and *Intolerance* (1916). These movies featured casts of thousands, forcing Griffith to devise new camera techniques in order to bring sweeping panoramas onto tiny screens.

The decade of the 1920s belonged to silent-screen stars such as William S. Hart, Mary Pickford, Buster Keaton, Charlie Chaplin, and Rudolph Valentino. The 1930s and 1940s were Hollywood's golden age. In 1939 alone, the musical fantasy *Wizard of Oz*, the

Glittering Hollywood, at one time the dream factory for all the world, still draws streams of visitors who want to remember the golden years.

exciting western movie *Stagecoach*, and the Civil War epic *Gone with the Wind* were produced.

Walt Disney launched his career by making ten-minute cartoon features in a Los Angeles garage. His creation of Mickey, the world's most-honored mouse, carried him to fame and riches. Disney's full-length animated movies *Pinocchio* (1940), *Fantasia* (1940), *Dumbo* (1941), *Bambi* (1942), and *Cinderella* (1950) are still praised as artistic, technical, and dramatic masterpieces.

During the late 1960s and early 1970s, the old Hollywood studios gradually lost their power to smaller, independent film companies. Few movies are made in Hollywood today, and the community is a shadow of its old self. But the town's history alone is enough to intrigue the streams of visitors who come each day to remember the time when glittering Hollywood was the dream factory for all the world.

SPORTS

The silvery beaches and sunny days of southern California invite swimming, surfing, sailboating, and deep-sea diving. Volleyball was invented in a gymnasium in Massachusetts, but Californians claim that the game grew popular along the beaches near Santa Barbara. In many spots, the sun-drenched beaches are just an hour's drive from the snow-topped Sierra Madres, where lovers of winter sports ski, bobsled, skate, and play ice hockey.

College basketball and college football are followed passionately in California. In the late 1960s and early 1970s, the University of California, Los Angeles (UCLA) basketball team won an incredible ten college championships. Two Los Angeles colleges, UCLA and the University of Southern California (USC), consistently produce powerhouse football teams.

In professional baseball, the Oakland A's assembled a powerful but cantankerous team in the early 1970s. The players fought with each other, yelled at reporters, and didn't get along with the team's owner. But they won three straight World Series. The San Diego Padres have had ups and downs, but they won the National League pennant in 1984. The Los Angeles Dodgers are perhaps the state's most popular sports attraction. Most of their games are played to a full stadium.

The state's strongest professional basketball team is the Los Angeles Lakers. Led by the ageless Kareem Abdul-Jabbar and the amazing 6 foot 9 inch guard Earvin "Magic" Johnson, the team won National Basketball Association (NBA) championships in 1982, 1985, and 1987.

The Los Angeles Rams, the San Francisco Forty-Niners, and the Los Angeles Raiders are traditionally strong professional football teams. The Forty-Niners were Super Bowl champions in 1982 and

Sports-minded Californians enjoy golfing at such beautiful courses as Pebble Beach (left), and hot-air ballooning in the Napa Valley (right).

1985. The San Diego Chargers win games with their sophisticated passing attack. The Raiders, famed and feared for their savagery on the field, moved from Oakland to Los Angeles in the early 1980s. The move enraged loyal Oakland fans, who began calling the team the "Traders."

Tennis courts are found everywhere, from the wealthiest suburbs to the inner-city neighborhoods. California has 695 golf courses. The most famous is the oceanside Pebble Beach course, on Monterey Bay's Seventeen-Mile Drive. Pebble Beach golfers often catch glimpses of whales playing in the surf. California's mania for sports includes unusual activities such as hot-air ballooning in the Napa Valley and hang gliding in the hill country.

Devotees of the rugged and exhilirating sport of rock climbing journey to Yosemite National Park to scale the lofty mountain called El Capitan. Standing three times taller than New York's Empire State Building, El Capitan is a sheer wall of granite with few ledges for toeholds. The climb takes three to five days to complete. At night, climbers sleep in narrow crevices and pray they will not roll over while dozing.

Chapter 9

HIGHLIGHTS OF THE GOLDEN STATE

HIGHLIGHTS OF THE GOLDEN STATE

To see all that California's cities and countryside have to offer would take a lifetime, but a brief tour might very well begin in the north.

THE NORTH COAST

In the coastal strip north of San Francisco are tiny villages, cool forest groves, and lonely beaches, many still undiscovered by tourists. Vacationers do come to this wildly beautiful region, but dozens of nooks and crannies go curiously unvisited. The north is nature's California; there is no big-city excitement here. Eureka, with twenty-four thousand people, and Redding, with forty-two thousand, are the largest population centers.

Almost touching the Oregon border is Redwood National Park, which stretches thirty miles (forty-eight kilometers) along the seashore. Here stand groves of majestic coastal redwoods. The world's tallest tree, a 368-foot (112-meter) giant, stands in this park. The town of Eureka is a logging center known for its splendid Victorian houses. Its most famous structure is an eighteen-room mansion built by lumber baron William Carson in the 1880s. The Carson house is a swirl of curlicues and wraparound balconies, all laced with gingerbread carvings.

South of Eureka, Highway 101 is called the Avenue of the Giants, as it cuts through more redwood country. The seaside

Eureka is a logging center known for its splendid Victorian houses. The most famous of these is the Carson House, built in the 1880s by lumber baron William Carson.

town of Mendocino looks as if it could be a Maine fishing village that was somehow moved to the Pacific coast. Founded in 1852 by new Englanders, Mendocino is now a popular hideaway for writers and artists.

Russian River country, an easy drive north from San Francisco, is a gentle blend of forests, hills, vineyards, and tumbling streams. It is one of the many regions along the north coast where a patient visitor can discover the perfect hidden spot to pitch a tent, take a hike, or sit and fish. And those who find a little garden of solitude along the north coast often say, "Shhhh, don't tell anyone else."

THE NORTHEAST

Even more sparsely populated than the north coast is the northeast corner's Cascade Range region. This area of untamed nature is dominated by snow-covered Mount Shasta. Indian legends mark the 14,000-foot (4,267-meter) mountain as the home of the Great Spirit.

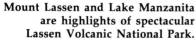

**Mount Lassen and Lake Manzanita
are highlights of spectacular
Lassen Volcanic National Park.**

Lassen Volcanic National Park, a highlight of the northeast, is a vast range of volcanic mountains, meadows, and clear lakes. The park's most prominent volcano, Mount Lassen, erupted violently in 1914. There has not been a major eruption for many years, but the region roils with underground thermal activity. Park visitors walk wooden plankways to get closeup views of steaming hot springs and bubbling pools of mud.

Sprawling Lake Tahoe lies south of Lassen Volcanic National Park. The lake offers swimming, fishing, and boating. Nature lovers hike the long and lonely trails along its southern banks. The nearby city of Truckee is a popular gathering point for skiers. Squaw Valley, the site of the 1960 Winter Olympic Games, is also nearby.

THE SIERRAS

The rugged "spine" of California presents some of the most breathtakingly beautiful land in all the world. Mark Twain wrote that the air in the Sierra peaks was "the same air the angels breathe."

Along the western face of the Sierras, opposite Sacramento, is Mother Lode Country. More than a century ago, gold fever brought an army of prospectors to this land. Occasional visitors still try their luck panning for gold in the streams. Those with sharp eyes and endless patience might even find specks of the yellow stuff. The best preserved of the old gold-mining towns is Columbia, where everything including the saloon's swinging doors has been carefully restored.

Crown jewel of the Sierras is Yosemite National Park. Spreading over 760,917 acres (307,932 hectares), its spectacular sights remain etched in the memory of the visitor forever. Guests at Yosemite hike its 700 miles (1,126 kilometers) of trails, raft on the Merced River, or swim in one of the park's 429 lakes. Mostly, though, visitors come to the Yosemite Valley to take in the awesome beauty of the massive rock walls and tumbling waterfalls.

To the south are Kings Canyon and Sequoia National Parks. Ancient glaciers carved out Kings Canyon's astonishing cliffs. Mount Whitney, the loftiest mountain in the continental United States, rises near the canyon. Sequoia National Park is the home of giant sequoia trees. Two of the park's trees—called General Sherman and General Grant—are among the largest trees in the world.

Mammoth Pool Reservoir is one of the Sierra's most popular recreation spots. In winter, it is a center for skiing, snowmobiling, and ice skating. In spring, schools of trout race through the lake and its many streams.

The only painful part of a trip to the Sierras is leaving. These lovely mountains have enchanted millions of visitors, including John Muir, who once wrote that "the Sierra should be called not the Nevada or the Snowy Range, but the Range of Light. It is the most divinely beautiful of all mountain chains I have ever seen."

In the Old Sacramento historical area, Gold Rush-era buildings have been restored and a statue has been erected to honor the Pony Express.

SACRAMENTO AND THE WINE COUNTRY

Grapes for wine making are grown in Sonoma County, in Livermore Valley, in the Central Valley, in Alexander Valley, and in the Russian River region. But the Napa Valley is the most famous wine country in the state. Like a giant grapevine, the valley twists north from the town of Napa. Its soil is rich, its days sunny, and its nights cool. Because of these conditions, Napa produces California's finest wines.

California's capital city, Sacramento, is both a center of political power and a gateway to the state's exciting past. In the heart of town is Old Sacramento, a twenty-eight-acre (eleven-hectare) historical area whose Gold Rush-era buildings have been restored. The wooden sidewalks, troughs, and hitching posts recall the days when horses and wagons were the main mode of transportation. A statue in Old Sacramento pays tribute to Theodore Judah, the engineer who pushed for the first transcontinental railroad. Another monument honors the Pony Express, whose western leg began in Sacramento in April 1860.

The Sacramento History Center presents the story of the Sacramento Valley from Indian times to the modern era. The nearby California State Railroad Museum delights train buffs. The fully reconstructed Sutter's Fort stands on its original site—within walking distance of downtown. Next door is the State Indian Museum, which contains many Native American artifacts. The Crocker Art Museum holds rare paintings collected by E. B. Crocker, brother of Charles Crocker, one of the state's powerful "Big Four" railroad tycoons. The Governor's Mansion, completed in 1878, is a Victorian-Gothic surprise for lovers of architecture.

THE BAY AREA

Approach the San Francisco Bay area from the north, and the magnificent Golden Gate Bridge greets you. This crown of the bay, which is painted in a color called "international orange," is one of America's most famous structures. In 1987, the Golden Gate celebrated its fiftieth birthday. The bridge is so well engineered that experts say it will stand for a thousand years. Near the bridge are Sausalito and Tiburon, two charming harbor towns known for their tasteful shops and chic cafes. Also a short drive from the bridge is Muir Woods, a splendid patch of forestland that includes a grove of coastal redwoods.

North of the Golden Gate, the Richmond-San Rafael Bridge links those two cities. From any of the bridges, San Francisco Bay looks like an enormous inland lake dotted with vessels ranging in size from tiny sailboats to gigantic aircraft carriers.

Oakland, San Francisco's sister city across the bay, is a busy transportation and shipping center. Lake Merritt, in the center of town, is a park complex that serves as the city's playground. On the shore of Lake Merritt is the excellent Oakland Museum, which

Lake Merritt, in the center of
Oakland, is a park complex that
serves as the city's playground.

specializes in California arts, history, and natural science. The
Mills College museum has a fine collection of art. Jack London
Square, on the waterfront, is a pleasant area for dining and
browsing among the nostalgic reminders of the 1890s, when Jack
London spent time here. Shoppers gravitate to nearby Jack
London Village or the Bret Harte Boardwalk.

At the south end of the bay are the cities of San Jose and Santa
Clara, and the high-tech industrial area called Silicon Valley. The
region produces silicon semiconductors, or chips, which are the
vital parts of any computer. The booming computer industry has
turned the southern bay into one of the wealthiest and fastest-
growing regions in the nation. Research facilities in nearby Palo
Alto and at Stanford University help keep the Silicon Valley
computer industry competitive with foreign producers.

From San Jose, the Bayshore Freeway leads north through Palo
Alto, Redwood City, Belmont, and finally to the soul of the Bay
Area—San Francisco.

Among famous San Francisco sights are Lombard Street (left), called the "crookedest street in the world"; Golden Gate Park (top), with its conservatory, museums, and gardens; and Ghirardelli Square (above), with its charming shops and restaurants.

The magic of San Francisco is felt in the zip of its winds and in the cool touch of the fog that rolls in from the ocean. Residents boast that it is everybody's favorite city. And they are right. Food lovers flock to Chinatown for the tastiest Oriental cuisine east of Hong Kong. Or they visit Fisherman's Wharf to sample an overwhelming variety of seafood. San Francisco's Palace of the Legion of Honor holds statues carved by Rodin and paintings by French Impressionists. Displays of Oriental art are featured at the M. H. de Young Memorial Museum. San Francisco has dozens of parks; the most popular is sprawling Golden Gate Park, with the exquisite Japanese Tea Gardens and still more museums.

San Francisco's glass-and-steel skyscrapers form a background for venerable Victorian row houses.

The town's forty hills, many of which are extremely steep, give rise to the old Bay Area saying, "When you get tired of walking around in San Francisco, you can always lean against it." To skirt the hills, people ride cable cars, those colorful relics of the past that San Franciscans refuse to give up. The city's architecture blends the old with the new. Gleaming glass-and-steel skyscrapers form a background for venerable Victorian row houses.

It is important to remember that San Franciscans harbor a fierce pride in their city and become annoyed when outsiders improperly shorten its name. So when visiting this monarch of the bay, never, never call it "Frisco."

The highlight of a visit to the Monterey Peninsula is a tour of Seventeen Mile Drive, with its cypress trees, dramatic ocean views, beautiful homes, and the famous Pebble Beach Golf Course. At Fishermen's Wharf in Monterey, shops and seafood restaurants line the tangle of wooden docks.

CENTRAL CALIFORNIA

Most trips along California's central coast begin at Santa Cruz, a resort city famed for its boardwalk and its muscular beach bums. Farther south is Monterey, a city steeped in history. Monterey served as the capital of Mexican California, and a few of its buildings, such as the waterfront Custom House, survive that era. Fishermen's Wharf in Monterey is a tangle of wooden docks lined with shops and seafood restaurants. It is also the home of the outstanding Monterey Bay Aquarium.

A popular coastal road, near Carmel, known as Seventeen Mile Drive, weaves through cliffs and groves of cypress trees. The Lone Cypress, a gnarled old tree growing out of a crevice in a cliff, is a popular tourist stop and is probably the most photographed tree in the state. A short drive away is trendy Carmel, with exclusive

Santa Cruz ●
● Fresno
Pfeiffer ● Monterey
Big Sur ● Carmel
State Park ● San Simeon
● Bakersfield
San Bernardino
National Forest
Santa Barbara ●
Riverside

One of the best times to visit Big Sur is in the spring, when wildflowers are in bloom.

shops and expensive restaurants. The city also boasts a marvelous beach, and one of the finest of California's original twenty-one missions. Father Junípero Serra, the founder of the mission system, is buried at Carmel.

Big Sur country is a 100-mile (161-kilometer) stretch of rugged cliffs, jagged hills, and lonely beaches between Carmel and San Simeon. A superb time to visit Big Sur is in the spring, when wildflowers color the countryside. The Hearst Castle at San Simeon was built by newspaper tycoon William Randolph Hearst in the 1920s. The architectural marvel contains priceless antiques and art objects collected from around the world. Now a state park, the Hearst Castle draws a million visitors a year.

An unmistakably Mexican look spreads through the city of Santa Barbara. White stucco houses with red-tiled roofs predominate, although each house looks subtly different from its neighbors. The Santa Barbara Court House has a striking Spanish design.

Inland from California's central coast spreads the flat and fertile San Joaquin Valley—the nation's fruit and vegetable basket. In the heart of the valley lies the city of Fresno. A leader in the packaging and processing of foods, Fresno produces about 80 percent of the nation's raisins. At the southern end of the San Joaquin Valley is the city of Bakersfield. Nearby oil fields spurred Bakersfield's growth early in the twentieth century, and today steel and cotton products are its major industries.

South of the San Joaquin Valley is mountainous country often called California's Inland Empire. Woodlands, including the San Bernardino National Forest, cover much of the area. Spectacular Lake Arrowhead is a magnet for many southern California vacationers. It was in the Inland Empire city of Riverside that a farmer named Tibbets planted two navel orange trees, which eventually grew into the state's billion-dollar citrus industry.

THE DESERTS

Death Valley National Monument lies in the southeast near the Nevada border. Its grim name is derived from the Gold Rush hopefuls who tried to cross its trackless wastes but died in the attempt. Today's visitors can tour a peculiar structure, Scotty's Castle, which was built by an eccentric millionaire named Death Valley Scotty.

The Indians who lived in the sandy lands along the lower Colorado River left some mysterious monuments of their own. On the desert floor they created pictures of men and beasts that are so huge they can be truly appreciated only when viewed from the heights of an airplane. In recent years, these enigmatic pictures have been scarred by thoughtless people joyriding over them on three-wheeled motorcycles.

Death Valley National Monument

Joshua Tree National Monument

Palm Springs •

Anza-Borrego Desert State Park

The fascinating variety of landscapes in California's desert areas include the sand dunes of Death Valley (left), the Joshua trees of the Joshua Tree National Monument (right), and the rugged beauty of Anza-Borrego Desert State Park.

The Joshua Tree National Monument features groves of Joshua trees, whose crooked limbs reminded Mormon travelers of the arms of the Biblical prophet Joshua beckoning them to the Promised Land. The Anza-Borrego Desert State Park spreads over the Sonora Desert. Herds of bighorn sheep are its star attraction, but only the most determined and patient nature lover will catch a glimpse of these shy animals.

A local newspaper writer claimed that in the resort city of Palm Springs "socializing is the number one industry." Located in the middle of the desert, the town is a winter home and playground for the rich. Thanks to irrigation, it has forty-two golf courses and a host of restaurants and nightclubs. More than fifteen thousand swimming pools grace its luxurious homes. Among Palm Springs' wealthy residents are Native Americans of the Cahuilla culture group, who are prominent landowners.

Traffic on the Harbor Freeway passes downtown Los Angeles (left). The city's many neighborhoods, which have the character of separate cities, are connected by a web of freeways.

LOS ANGELES AND SAN DIEGO

Los Angeles has been called "a hundred suburbs in search of a city." Rambling neighborhoods such as Westwood, Malibu, Hollywood, and a dozen more spread out over its 460 square miles (1,191 square kilometers). The neighborhoods, which have the character of separate cities, are connected by a web of freeways.

Much of downtown Los Angeles is dominated by modern, rather faceless towers, but older buildings harbor architectural surprises. The Bradley Building, erected in 1893, appears unexciting on the outside, but the inside contains a marvelous staircase made of carved wood and Oriental ironwork. The stunning granite-finished City Hall is Los Angeles' most familiar landmark. Standing twenty-six stories tall, it was for years the tallest structure in town. After construction improvements made tall buildings earthquake-safe, laws passed in the 1950s permitted high-rise buildings. The Los Angeles Public Library's flowing Spanish lines stop strollers on the street and invite them to take a closer look.

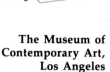

Los Angeles
Anaheim
Newport Beach
San Diego

**The Museum of
Contemporary Art,
Los Angeles**

Visitors to the Los Angeles area may tour Universal Studios and recall the days when Hollywood was the movie capital of the world. The gigantic Hollywood Bowl seats twenty thousand people for its outdoor summertime concerts. Fine pieces of modern art are displayed at the Museum of Contemporary Art and the Los Angeles County Museum of Art. The city also has excellent natural history and science museums.

South of Los Angeles spreads Orange County. It, too, is a sea of suburbs, but it also boasts superb beaches such as Laguna, Newport, and Balboa. And in Orange County lies the dreamland for children everywhere.

In a tiny village in Mexico, a teacher asked her class which place they would most like to visit in the entire United States. Altogether, the boys and girls chimed, *"Disneylandia!"* Such is the international fame of Disneyland, the fantastic theme park in the city of Anaheim. Disneyland opened in 1955. Since then, the Burbank-based Disney Corporation has opened similar parks in Orlando, Florida, and Tokyo, Japan. But in the minds of people

San Diego
Harbor at
day's end

everywhere, the Anaheim park remains the true home of the
Wonderful World of Disney.

The list of things to do in San Diego is impressive. Visitors may
stroll through the San Diego Zoo, one of the world's largest and
most innovative. They can lunch at the Hotel del Coronado, an
architectural wonder on Coronado Island. Many stop at Sea World
to watch the amazing performance of dolphins. Or they study the
history of shipping at the Maritime Museum. In Balboa Park are
the famed Museum of Man, and other museums devoted to
history, natural history, aerospace, and sports. Finally, the miles
of parkland that ring San Diego's waterfront invite long walks.
When the sun sets over the sailboats bobbing in the bay, visitors
discover what San Diegans have long been sure of—theirs is the
prettiest city in southern California.

San Diego, which hugs the Mexican border, marks the end of
many tours of California. The Golden State is the most powerful,
the most populous, and the most exciting of American states. Yet
it is much more. For millions of people, it will always remain a
place to fulfill dreams.

FACTS AT A GLANCE

GENERAL INFORMATION

Statehood: September 9, 1850; thirty-first state

Origin of Name: Named by Spanish explorers after *California,* the mythical island paradise in Garci Ordonez de Montalvo's sixteenth-century book, *Las Sergas de Esplandian*

State Capital: Sacramento

State Nickname: Golden State

State Flag: The state flag, adopted in 1911, was first raised in California during the Bear Flag Revolt of 1846 by settlers rebelling against Mexican rule. The flag shows a white field with a grizzly bear standing on a patch of green grass above the words "California Republic"; there is a red star in the upper left-hand corner and a red stripe across the bottom.

State Motto: *Eureka,* or "I have found it"

State Bird: California valley quail

State Animal: California grizzly bear

State Marine Mammal: California gray whale

State Insect: California dog-face butterfly

State Fish: Golden trout

State Flower: Golden poppy

State Tree: California redwood

State Mineral: Native gold

State Rock: Serpentine

State Fossil: Saber-toothed cat

State Song: "I Love You, California," words by F.B. Silverwood, music by A.F. Frankenstein; adopted in 1951:

I love you, California, you're the greatest state of all;
I love you in the winter, summer, spring, and in fall;
I love your fertile valleys; your dear mountains I adore;
I love your grand old ocean and I love her rugged shore.

Chorus:
Where the snow-crowned Golden Sierras
Keep their watch o'er the valleys bloom,
It is there I would be in our land by the sea,
Ev'ry breeze bearing rich perfume,
It is here nature gives of her rarest
It is Home Sweet Home to Me,
And I know when I die I shall breath my last sigh
For my sunny California.

I love your redwood forests—love your fields of yellow grain;
I love your summer breezes and I love your winter rain;
I love you, land of flowers; land of honey, fruit and wine;
I love you, California; you have won this heart of mine.

(Chorus)

I love your old gray Missions—love your vineyards stretching far;
I love you, California, with your Golden Gate ajar;
I love your purple sunsets, love your skies of azure blue;
I love you, California; I just can't help loving you.

(Chorus)

I love you, California, you are very dear to me;
I love you, Tamalpais, and I love Yosemite;
I love you, Land of Sunshine, Half your beauties are untold;
I loved you in my childhood, and I'll love you when I'm old.

(Chorus)

POPULATION

Population: 29,760,021, first among the states (1990 census)

Population Density: 188 people per sq. mi. (72 people per km²)

Population Distribution: 91 percent of California's people live in cities or towns. Los Angeles, California's most-populated city, ranked second in population size in the United States. Nearly thirty percent of the state's population (8,863,164) lives in the Los Angeles-Long Beach metropolitan area, which is California's largest metropolitan area. Forty-six other California cities have populations over 100,000, including San Diego, sixth largest city in the nation; San Jose, eleventh in the nation; and San Francisco, fourteenth in the nation.

Los Angeles	3,485,398
San Diego	1,110,549
San Jose	782,248
San Francisco	723,959
Long Beach	429,433
Oakland	372,242
Sacramento	369,365
Fresno	354,202
Santa Ana	293,742
Anaheim	266,406

(Population figures according to 1990 census)

Population Growth: California's population increased rapidly from statehood in 1850 through the 1980s. Between 1890 and 1970, California's population nearly doubled every twenty years, and in 1970, California replaced New York as the nation's most-populous state. From 1980 to 1990, California's population increased by nearly 26 percent, while the population of the entire country increased 9.8 percent. The list below gives the population figures for California since statehood:

Year	Population
1850	92,597
1860	379,994
1880	864,964
1900	1,485,053
1920	3,426,861
1940	6,907,387
1950	10,586,223
1960	15,717,204
1970	19,971,069
1980	23,667,826
1990	29,760,021

Native Americans: California's Native American population is 242,164, 0.8 percent of the state's population.

GEOGRAPHY

Borders: States that border California are Oregon on the north, Nevada on the east, and Arizona (separated from California by the Colorado River) on the southeast. Baja California (Mexico) determines California's southern boundary. The Pacific Ocean determines California's western boundary.

Highest Point: Mount Whitney, 14,494 ft. (4,418 m), also the highest point in the contiguous United States

Lowest Point: Death Valley, 282 ft. (86 m) below sea level, also the lowest point in the continental United States

Greatest Distances: North to south—770 mi. (1,239 km)
East to west—360 mi. (579 km)

Area: 158,693 sq. mi. (411,013 km²)

Rank in Area Among the States: Third

Rivers: California's two major rivers are the Sacramento, which flows south through the Central Valley, and the San Joaquin, which flows northwest through the Central Valley; they meet northeast of San Francisco and flow together westward into San Francisco Bay. Important tributaries of the Sacramento are the Pit, McCloud, Feather, and American rivers; tributaries of the San Joaquin include the Stanislaus, Tuolumne, and Merced rivers. These two river systems drain most of northern California and the interior Central Valley. The Klamath and its main tributary, the Trinity, along with the Mad, Eel, and Russian rivers also provide important drainage in northern California. Southern California's many rivers are noted for disappearing in summer heat, either from evaporation or, like Death Valley's Amargosa River, by retreating beneath the surface of the land. In the rainy season, however, these rivers may become raging torrents that cause serious floods. The Santa Ana and the Santa Clara are two of southern California's important rivers. The Colorado River, which forms the state's southeastern boundary, provides water for Los Angeles and other southern California cities as well as irrigation water for desert farmlands.

Lakes: California has about 8,000 natural and man-made lakes or reservoirs. The shallow, salty Salton Sea is the state's largest saltwater lake; it formed in 1905 when the Colorado River flooded into an ancient lake bottom in the Imperial Valley. Lake Tahoe, shared by California and Nevada, is the state's deepest and largest lake. California's major reservoirs are the Shasta, on the Sacramento River; the Oroville, on the Feather River; the Trinity, on the Trinity River; the New Melones, on the Stanislaus River; and the Folsom, on the American River.

Topography: California's topography is the battle-scarred face of a land that experienced millenia of flooding by ancient seas, the heaving and buckling of mountain formation, and the scouring of glacial ice sheets on the move.

Today, the Central Valley, or Great Valley, is the state's most-distinctive topographic feature. The Central Valley is a mostly level plain, averaging 50 mi. (80 km) in width and extending northwest to southeast for almost 430 mi. (692 km) in length. It contains three-fifths of California's farmland, the most fertile land west of the Rocky Mountains, and occupies one-sixth of the state's total land. The valley is hemmed in by a mountainous region in the north, the Sierra Nevada Range on the east, and the Coast Ranges on the west. The San Francisco Bay area, where the Sacramento and San Joaquin Rivers flow to the Pacific Ocean, is the only gap in the mountain walls surrounding the Central Valley.

California's rugged mountainous region north of the Central Valley consists of the Klamath Mountains and the Cascade Mountains, including the still-active

Palm Canyon, Anza-Borrega State Park

volcano, Lassen Peak, and the now-dormant volcano, glacier-topped Mount Shasta.

The Sierra Nevada range extends south from the Cascades, forming a high wall that acts as the Central Valley's eastern border. Many of California's highest peaks are in the Sierras. Mount Whitney, the state's highest point at 14,494 ft. (4,418 m), is part of this range. Two million years ago, glaciers were at work reshaping the Sierras: they carved out deep valleys and towering walls over which great waterfalls rush; they created glacial lakes and rolled out flat meadow areas. Yosemite National Park, in the midsection of the Sierras, boasts several of North America's highest waterfalls: Ribbon Falls, Upper Yosemite, and Silver Strand. Lake Tahoe, high in the Sierras, is one of California's—and the nation's—most popular vacation spots.

The Central Valley's western wall is formed by the Coast Ranges, a general name for several mountain chains that stand parallel to the California coastline. The Coast Ranges proper extend from the Klamath Mountains in the north at Cape Mendocino to Point Conception in the south at Santa Barbara County. South of Point Conception is a complex of narrow ranges commonly considered part of the Coast Ranges. Included are the Los Angeles Ranges, also called the Transverse Ranges, and the San Diego Ranges, sometimes called the Peninsular Ranges. Valleys within the Coast Ranges include the beautiful Napa Valley north of San Francisco and the Santa Clara, Salinas, and San Fernando valleys to the south. The San Andreas Fault is a break in the earth's crust along which earthquakes arise; it enters California from the Pacific near Point Arena in the north and follows the Coast Ranges into southern California. Many other fault lines crisscross the state.

The northeastern corner of California and a large expanse of southeastern California belong to the Great Basin and Range region of the United States, which extends east into Nevada, north into Oregon, and outward to several other states. California's northeastern corner, hemmed in by steep ranges, is a lava-bed plateau, or "high-desert" area. In California's southeast, Death Valley, in the low-lying Basin and Range region, contains the state's lowest point. The Mojave and

Colorado deserts, called the low deserts, also lie in the southeast. Some arid desert lands have been reclaimed for farming by irrigation, resulting in the fertile Imperial and Coachella valleys.

Sandwiched between the Coast Ranges and the Pacific Ocean is a narrow band of coastline that extends from the rocky headlands of northern California to the low, sandy, beaches of the south. The coastline is interrupted by San Francisco Bay, one of the world's largest natural harbors, and by bays at San Diego, Humboldt, and Monterey. A major artificial harbor has been created at Los Angeles. Two island groups lie offshore: the small Farallon Islands are west of San Francisco; the Channel, or Santa Barbara, Islands, including popular Catalina Island, are in southern California.

Climate: California's climate varies with its topography; moderate temperatures and rainfall occur along the densely populated coast, while extremes occur in the interior. Coastal summers and winters are mild; Los Angeles has an annual average temperature of 65° F. (18.3° C), with an average January low of 47° F. (8.3° C) and an average July high of 83° F. (28.3° C). San Francisco has an annual average temperature of 57° F. (13.9° C), with January lows averaging 46° F. (7.8° C) and July highs averaging 65° F. (18.3° C). Away from the coast, mountainous regions experience milder summers but colder winters; the Central Valley has hot summers with cool winters; and the Imperial Valley experiences very hot and dry summers. The highest recorded temperature in California, and the highest ever in the nation, was 134° F. (56.7° C) at Greenland Ranch in Death Valley on July 10, 1913. California's lowest recorded temperature was -45° F. (-42.8° C) at Boca, near Lake Tahoe, on January 20, 1937.

Most of California experiences just two seasons, one dry and the other wet. Annual precipitation in the state varies from 2 in. (5 cm) in the Imperial Valley to 68 in. (173 cm) at Crescent City. Along the coast, heavy fog is common during the summer months and tropical rainstorms during the winter months; inland in the Central Valley, rains alternate with "tule fog" in the winter; San Francisco averages 21 in. (54 cm) of annual precipitation, while Los Angeles averages 15 in. (38 cm). Weather extremes in the state achieved two national records: the longest rainless period, 760 days in Death Valley's Bagdad (October 3, 1912 to November 8, 1914), and the largest one-month snowfall, 390 in. (991 cm) in Alpine County (January 1911).

NATURE

Trees: Cedar, fir, hemlock, California laurel (bay), maple, cottonwood, oak, pine, redwood, spruce; the Peruvian pepper tree and many varieties of Australian eucalyptus have naturalized within the state

Wild Plants: California's arid zone supports a large variety of plants, including asters, desert evening primrose, dwarf desert poppy, sand verbena, Joshua tree, cactus varieties, creosote bush, indigo bush, and juniper bush, as well as shrubs of mesquite, buttonweed, and sagebrush. Valley and mountain-slope plants include alumroot, barrenwort, beard-tongue, California (or golden) poppy, evening primrose, ferns, fireweed, lilies, lupine varieties, mariposa, phacelia, trillium, tulip, viola, and shrubs of azalea, blackberry, currant, elderberry, and huckleberry. Alpine plants include Sierra primrose, yellow columbine, alpine buttercup, and alpine shootingstar; alpine shrubs include dwarf manzanita and ceanothus.

Animals: Some four hundred species of mammals live in California, including bears, bobcats, ring-tailed cats, cougars, coyotes, deer, elk, foxes, mountain lions, mink, muskrat, mountain sheep, weasels, and wolverines. The state's arid and semi-arid regions are home to pronghorned antelope, jackrabbit, kangaroo rats, opossums, squirrels, horned toads, desert tortoises, and several kinds of snakes. Seals and sea lions live off the coast of California, and whales are seen offshore.

Birds: California's six hundred species of birds include the nearly extinct California condor, as well as bluebirds, mourning doves, ducks, geese, grouse, hawks, jays, juncos, owls, quails, thrashers, thrush, turkeys, and cactus wrens.

Fish: Freshwater fish include bass, salmon, catfish, sunfish, sturgeon, and trout; coastal and marine varieties include deep-sea rockfish, bass, perch, tuna, barracuda, marlin, and abalone, as well as clams, crabs, oysters, scallops, shrimps, and other shellfish.

GOVERNMENT

The government of California, like that of the federal government, is divided into three branches—legislative, executive, and judicial. The legislature consists of a forty-member senate and an eighty-member assembly. The legislature writes new laws, repeals or revises old laws, and works with the governor to prepare the state budget. Senators are elected to four-year terms and members of the assembly to two-year terms.

The executive branch is headed by the governor, whose task is to administer the law. The governor is elected to a four-year term; there is no limit to the number of terms a governor may serve. The state constitution gives the governor the power and responsibility to approve or veto laws passed by the legislature, to serve as commander-in-chief of the state militia, and to call emergency sessions of the legislature. Other elected members of the executive branch include the lieutenant governor, secretary of state, attorney general, treasurer, and the superintendent of public education. All are elected to four-year terms.

The judicial branch interprets laws and tries cases. The state has three kinds of courts—supreme, appellate, and trial. The supreme court is the state's highest court; it has a chief justice and six associate justices. There are six district courts of appeal, with a total of seventy-seven justices. Justices of the supreme court and the district courts of appeal are appointed by the governor; the appointments are then subject to voter approval. These justices serve twelve-year terms. Each county has one superior court, whose judges are elected to six-year terms. The lower courts consist of municipal and justice courts. Judicial districts with more than forty-thousand people have municipal courts; those with fewer than forty-thousand people have justice courts.

University of
California at
Santa Cruz

In addition, the state's constitution allows California citizens to pass laws directly under a system known as initiative. If 5 percent of the people who voted in the previous election sign a petition favoring a proposed law, that proposition will be put on the next general-election ballot. If the voters approve the proposition, it becomes law. Under a system called referendum, California voters have the right to challenge a law passed by the legislature. If 5 percent of the people who voted in the previous election challenge a proposed law, that law will not go into effect unless it is approved by voters in the next general election.

Number of Counties: 58

U.S. Representatives: 45

Electoral Votes: 47

Voting Qualifications: Eighteen years of age, thirty days residency

EDUCATION

California's 1849 state constitution called for a statewide public-school system. Legislation in 1866 assured sufficient tax funds to support free elementary schools, and a 1903 law extended tax support to public high schools. California's first tax-supported school, financed by the city of San Francisco, opened in 1850. The nation's first tax-supported junior college opened in Fresno in 1910. Today, elementary and public-school education in California is under the control of an eleven-member state board of education. There are about 1,029 public school districts, with an enrollment of more than 4 million students. In addition, another 540,000 students, about 13 percent of all students, are enrolled in private schools; of students attending private schools, approximately 76 percent attend schools that are religiously oriented. Children are required to attend school from the age of six to eighteen, unless they graduate sooner, or are admitted to a college or university by means of a special examination.

California has the nation's largest system of state colleges and universities. The University of California has its main campus at Berkeley and branches at Davis,

Irvine, Los Angeles (UCLA), Riverside, San Diego, San Francisco, Santa Barbara, and Santa Cruz. The California State University system has nineteen campuses and there are many state community colleges. Among the noted private colleges and universities in California are the University of Southern California in Los Angeles; the California Institute of Technology in Pasadena; Mills College in Oakland; Occidental College in Los Angeles; the University of the Pacific in Stockton; Pepperdine University in Malibu; the University of San Francisco; the University of Santa Clara; Whittier College; the University of San Diego; Stanford University; and Pomona, Claremont Graduate School, Scripps, Claremont McKenna, Pitzer, and Harvey Mudd at Claremont.

Specialized advanced studies are pursued at private institutions such as the Center for Advanced Study in the Behavioral Science at Palo Alto; the Center for the Study of Democratic Institutions at Santa Barbara; and the Rand Corporation at Santa Monica. Observatories at Mount Wilson, near Pasadena, and Mount Palomar, in northern San Diego County, are jointly sponsored by the Carnegie Institution and the California Institute of Technology. Major research centers of the University of California include Lick Observatory, east of San Jose, the Lawrence Radiation Laboratory at Livermore, and the Scripps Institute of Oceanography at La Jolla.

ECONOMY AND INDUSTRY

Principal Products:
Agriculture: Dairy products, beef cattle, grapes, nursery products, cotton, hay, rice, flowers and foliage, lettuce, almonds, tomatoes for processing, strawberries, oranges, eggs, chickens, broccoli, turkeys, walnuts, sugar beets, peaches, potatoes, avocados, olives, garlic, pears, plums, nectarines, cherries, melons, lemons
Manufacturing: Foods, wines, primary and fabricated metals, machinery, electric and electronic equipment, computers, computer software, chemicals and allied products, printed materials, petroleum, textiles, aircraft, missiles, automobiles and trucks, shipbuilding
Natural Resources: Timber (fir, pine, redwood, oak), cement, boron minerals, sand and gravel, crushed stone, tuna fish, crabs

Business and Trade: Service industries are California's fastest-growing business sector. Services to business include insurance, real estate, data processing, and others; consumer services include health and personal services as well as recreation and amusement services. Los Angeles is a leading trade center and the major wholesale distribution center on the West Coast. San Francisco also is a center for wholesale and international trade. Chevron, headquartered in San Francisco, and Atlantic Richfield, with headquarters in Los Angeles, are the top publicly held corporations in California; both specialize in petroleum products. Led by growth in consumer and commercial electronics, aerospace, and defense, California's economy is currently growing faster than that of the nation as a whole. Northern California's Silicon Valley is the center of high-tech computer and computer-related businesses.

Nearly 100 million tourists and travelers visit California each year. They contribute about $26 billion to the state's economy—including nearly 4 percent of the state's total tax revenue—and generate more than 500,000 jobs in various tourist services. Southern California is a leading center of motion-picture production. The motion-picture industry was also responsible for the growth of television production in the Los Angeles and San Francisco areas, and the sports-clothing and high-style apparel industry of Los Angeles.

Communication: There are 63 commercial and 13 non-commercial television stations in California. In addition, there are 237 AM radio stations, 243 FM radio stations, and 84 educational radio stations. Only Texas has a greater number of television and AM radio stations, and no other state has more FM radio stations or more cable-television subscribers. About 840 newspapers are published in California, including 600 weeklies and 130 dailies. The most important papers are the *Los Angeles Times*, the *San Francisco Chronicle*, the *Orange County Register*, the *Los Angeles Herald Examiner*, the *Sacramento Bee*, and the *San Jose Mercury-News*. California prints a larger number of newspapers than any other state; the state ranks fourth in the nation in book and periodical publishing.

Transportation: A network of 175,000 mi. (281,635 km) of roads and highways crisscross California; two-thirds of these are surfaced. The Golden Gate Bridge in San Francisco, one of the most famous bridges in the world, links San Francisco with Marin County; the two other bridges that cross San Francisco Bay are the San Francisco-Oakland Bridge and the Richmond-San Rafael Bridge.

California has more than 280 public airports; the International Airports at Los Angeles and San Francisco are among the nation's busiest. Other major California airports include those at San Diego, San Jose, Oakland, and Ontario. Thirty-four railroads operate on about 6,900 mi. (11,000 km) track. There is passenger service between about forty of California's cities.

The major seaports in southern California are at Los Angeles, Long Beach, and San Diego. In northern California, the San Francisco Bay area ships millions of tons of cargo yearly from the deep-water ports of San Francisco, Oakland, Redwood City, and Richmond. Sacramento and Stockton are important inland ports; they are connected to San Francisco by deep-water channels and handle shipments of agricultural, forest, and mineral products from the Sacramento and San Joaquin valleys.

SOCIAL AND CULTURAL LIFE

Museums: The M.H. de Young Memorial Museum, one of three museums located in San Francisco's Golden Gate Park, exhibits paintings by European and African artists and cultural artifacts created by early American Indians. The Asian Art Museum, in the west wing of the de Young Museum, contains an extensive collection of oriental jade and porcelain. The California Academy of Sciences is home to many smaller museums of natural history. Also in San Francisco is the California Palace of the Legion of Honor, which exhibits a fine collection of French Impressionist paintings and sculpture. In Los Angeles, the Norton Simon Museum presents works of European masters. The Southwest Museum, also in Los Angeles, is noted for its superb collection of southwestern Native American art. The California Museum of Science and Industry, the Los Angeles County Natural

History Museum, and the Museum of Afro-American History and Culture are all located in Exposition Park in Los Angeles. The Fisher Gallery, at the University of Southern California, houses the Armand Hammer collection of eighteenth- and nineteenth-century Dutch paintings. The Huntington Library, Art Gallery, and Botanical Garden in San Marino are located on the former estate of the rail tycoon. The J. Paul Getty Museum, in Malibu, contains an excellent art library and noteworthy holdings of ancient Greek and Roman art. San Diego boasts twenty-three museums, including the Timben Art Gallery, the Serra Museum, and the Reuben H. Fleet Space Theater and Science Center. The Crocker Art Museum in Sacramento is the oldest public art museum in the West, and among the most important.

The state, counties, cities, and universities of California maintain hundreds of publicly funded museums, gardens, and zoos. Among these are the Los Angeles Zoo; Marineland, a seaside zoo; and the world-famous San Diego Zoo.

Libraries: California has about 170 main public libraries and nearly 600 branch libraries, containing more than 46 million volumes. The Los Angeles Public Library system is the state's largest. San Francisco and San Diego also have extensive public library holdings. The University of California at Berkeley has one of the nation's leading research libraries and is the state's largest university library. In addition, its Bancroft Library collection of rare materials on the American West is outstanding. At Stanford and UCLA are top-rated research libraries. The University of California campuses at Davis, San Diego, Santa Barbara, Riverside, and Irvine have large collections. Among private libraries, the Huntington Library in San Marino counts rare and priceless books and manuscripts as entries in its catalog.

Performing Arts: The Los Angeles Philharmonic and the San Francisco Symphony orchestras are among the nation's prestigious symphonic ensembles. San Francisco and San Diego each have a resident world-class opera company. There is a resident ballet company in San Francisco and one in Oakland. Los Angeles is noted for the Los Angeles City Ballet and is the western home of the Joffrey Ballet. In addition to these outstanding institutions, 47 other symphony orchestras call California home, as do 15 other opera companies, 18 classical choral groups, and 220 additional dance companies. The annual Monterey Jazz Festival attracts thousands of enthusiastic listeners, and the Hollywood Bowl in Los

Angeles seats twenty thousand for outdoor concerts. Also in Los Angeles is the Mark Taper Forum, a theater-in-the-round that is noted for its repertory company. Major theatrical productions are staged at the Westwood Playhouse near the UCLA campus, and the Pantages Theater on Hollywood Boulevard, both also in Los Angeles. In San Francisco, the American Conservatory Theater performs classical and modern plays at the Geary Theater; Broadway musicals are performed at the Curran Theater, the Little Fox Theater, the On-Broadway Theater, and the Club Fugazi. In San Diego, the Old Globe Theater stages a Shakespearean festival every summer and the Mission Playhouse does classic, modern, and experimental plays.

Sports and Recreation: California cheers for more home professional sports teams than any other state: the Golden State is home to five major-league baseball teams, four professional football teams, four professional basketball teams, and a professional hockey team. The Los Angeles Dodgers, the San Francisco Giants, and the San Diego Padres baseball teams all play in the National League. The Oakland Athletics and the California Angels are members of the American League. California has four National Football League teams: The San Francisco Forty Niners, the Los Angeles Rams, the Los Angeles Raiders, and the San Diego Chargers. California's National Basketball Association teams include the Los Angeles Lakers, the Los Angeles Clippers, the Golden State Warriors, and the Sacramento Kings. The Los Angeles Kings belong to the National Hockey League. In college sports, traditional powerhouses include UCLA in basketball and UCLA, Stanford, and the University of Southern California in football. Other major sports attractions include the Bob Hope Desert Classic in golf, and the Annual Rose Bowl Tournament held on New Year's Day at Pasadena. Major horse-racing tracks include those at Santa Anita, Hollywood Park, Del Mar, and Bay Meadows.

With its varied topography, vast coastline, and mild climate, California provides many opportunities for year-round outdoor sports and recreation. More than one-fourth of California's land area is devoted to national and state recreational areas. There are five national parks, twenty-two national forests, twenty-two natural wildlife refuges, and the Point Reyes National Seashore north of San Francisco. The state park system operates nearly two hundred parks, beaches, reserves, and historic sites. From boating, fishing, hang gliding, and surfing along the coast, to off-road motoring in the desert, to backpacking and mountain climbing in the Sierras, California can provide for nearly every conceivable sports and recreational activity.

Historic Sites and Landmarks:

Alcatraz Island, in San Francisco Bay, is now a part of the Golden Gate National Recreational Area. Alcatraz was the island prison from which no one is known to have successfully escaped; it was a military prison housing conscientious objectors during World War I; from 1934 to 1963, it was a maximum-security federal penitentiary with infamous prisoners such as Al Capone and "Machine Gun" Kelly.

The Cabrillo National Monument, on the Point Loma Promontory, celebrates San Diego's discoverer, Juan Rodríguez Cabrillo. A statue of the explorer, presented by the Portuguese government, faces the site of his landing.

Death Valley National Monument has changing desert landscapes that include such natural wonders as Badwater, the lowest point in the United States, and Artist's Palette, where the rocks have oxidized into shades of green, blue, purple, red, and yellow. The passage of pioneers and settlers through the desert is recorded in ghost towns, abandoned gold mines, and Scotty's Castle, the luxurious mansion constructed by eccentric millionaire "Death Valley Scotty."

El Pueblo de Los Angeles, a state historic park within the city, preserves California's Spanish and Mexican heritage; in the park are the century-old Moreton Bay fig trees in the Old Plaza, the Avila Adobe, the Pico House (a once-famous hotel), and the Plaza Church.

Hearst Castle, near San Luis Obispo at San Simeon, was built by newspaper publisher William Randolph Hearst during the 1920s and now is a state historic park. It is an architectural wonderment that includes a castle with many art works, a Roman temple, a private theater, and huge swimming pools.

Inyo National Forest's Bristlecone Pines, on the eastern slope of the Sierras, are estimated to be 4,600 years old, the oldest living things on earth.

Joshua Tree National Monument, where the Mojave and Colorado deserts meet, has Joshua trees that reach heights of 50 feet (15 meters). Indians used them for food, medicine, and fiber; Mormons saw in their crooked branches the arms of the Biblical Joshua pointing to the Promised Land.

La Brea Tar Pits, in Los Angeles' Hancock Park, was an Ice Age death trap, luring birds and animals to drink in the shallow pools, then sucking them down to be entombed in the tar pits below. The nearby Page Museum of La Brea Discoveries displays skeletons of the one million mammal and bird fossils excavated from the site along with fossilized plants and insects.

Mission Basilica San Carlos Borromeo del Rio Carmelo, at Carmel, was founded at Monterey in 1770 and moved to Carmel in 1771. Franciscan Father Junípero Serra and more than twenty-three hundred Indians associated with the mission are buried there.

Mission Basilica San Diego de Alcalá, in San Diego, was founded in 1769. It was the first of California's twenty-one Franciscan missions, and moved to its present site in 1774. Still an active parish church, it includes a chapel, garden courtyard, and the restored living quarters of Father Junípero Serra, its founder.

Mission San Juan Capistrano, founded in 1776, was the seventh mission of Franciscan Father Junípero Serra. The original Great Stone Church, destroyed by earthquake, has been reproduced. The Serra Chapel, built in 1777, is California's oldest building.

Muir Woods National Monument, a redwood forest just minutes north of San Francisco, honors naturalist John Muir.

**Disneyland and Hollywood
are two of the favorite
attractions for visitors
to the Los Angeles area.**

Other Interesting Places to Visit

Big Sur, the 100-mile- (161-kilometer-) long stretch of coast from Monterey south to San Luis Obispo, offers breathtaking views to travelers along Route 1, the scenic highway that often clings only to a narrow ledge that was blasted out of the cliffs.

Columbia, in the Sierra foothills, offers one of the state's best representations of a Gold Rush town.

Disneyland, in Anaheim, is the first theme park designed by Walt Disney. Opened in 1955, the park features re-creations of tropical jungles, the Wild West, and a turn-of-the-century small American town.

Hollywood, now a district within the city of Los Angeles, is still considered the center of the world's motion-picture industry. Movies and television shows still are made there, and tram tours still pack in tourists at Universal Studios. Handprints, footprints, and some pawprints of the stars of the 1920s and 1930s are impressed into the cement courtyard of Mann's (formerly Grauman's) Chinese Theater.

Knott's Berry Farm, in Buena Park, is the state's oldest amusement-theme park. The theme is the Old West, with stagecoach rides, burros, and a mine train, as well as performances by popular Country and Western artists.

Marineland, at Palos Verdes Estates, is a gigantic aquatic-theme park stocked with representative sea life. One way to tour Marineland is to swim through in rented mask, fins, and snorkel.

Redwood Highway (U.S. 101) passes through groves of the world's tallest trees, the redwoods, on its way from San Francisco north to Oregon.

Ribbon Falls, in Yosemite national park, is the highest waterfall in the United States at 1,612 feet (491 meters). Other beautiful waterfalls, peaceful meadows, and soaring peaks lie within Yosemite, one of the nation's oldest national parks.

The San Diego Zoo, in Balboa Park, is one of the world's most respected zoos; large collections of birds, reptiles, and mammals are cared for and displayed in simulated natural habitats.

San Francisco, which calls itself "Everybody's Favorite City," features cable car rides; a Chinatown that encompasses the largest Chinese community in the United States; Fisherman's Wharf on the waterfront; Golden Gate Bridge; and shopping at Ghirardelli Square, an old chocolate factory that has been converted into boutiques and specialty shops.

The State Capitol in Sacramento, has been restored to its 1910 days of glory with muted pastel colors and a dome of gold leaf. Nearby are the restored Governor's Mansion and the reconstructed site of Sutter's Fort.

Wine Country in California includes the Napa and Sonoma Valleys, the Russian River region, and Paso Robles in San Luis Obispo County. Many of the wineries offer tours of the vineyard and tastes of the product.

IMPORTANT DATES

c. 10,000 B.C.—Prehistoric Indians populate California; coastal groups subsist on fish and sea mammals; other groups rely on the acorn as a staple food; in non-coastal areas, living patterns are influenced by natural resources at hand; farming techniques are practiced where appropriate or necessary

A.D. 1500s—California's Indian population before European contact (estimated at 150,000-300,000) include Hupa in the northeast, Maidu in the center, Yuma in the south, and smaller groups of Pomo, Miwok, Modoc, and Mojave

1542—Juan Rodríguez Cabrillo explores the coast of California for Spain

1579—Francis Drake lands on California coast and takes possession of the land for England

1602—Sebastían Vizcaíno surveys Monterey Bay area as possible site for a Spanish Colony

1769—Spanish colonization begins at San Diego with the founding of the first of twenty-one California missions, San Diego de Alcalá, by Franciscan priest Junipero Serra and the first presidio (military fort) by Captain Gaspar de Portolá, Governor of Baja California

1776—Juan Bautista de Anza leads overland expedition to select the site for settlement on San Francisco Bay; Spanish settlers from New Spain (Mexico) arrive at San Francisco (then known as Yerba Buena)

1781—Spain establishes a colony at Los Angeles

1812—Russians establish Fort Ross (Sonoma County) north of San Francisco

1822—Province of California declares allegiance to New Spain (Mexico), which had gained independence from Spain in 1821

1841—John Bidwell and John Bartleson lead the first organized group of American settlers, from Missouri, to reach California by land

1842-46—John C. Frémont leads United States government expeditions into California

1846—Frémont raises the United States flag over Hawk's Peak, near Monterey, but withdraws; the United States and Mexico go to war two months later; American settlers capture the Mexican fort at Sonoma and raise the Bear Flag of the California Republic

1848—Mexico cedes California to the United States under the Treaty of Guadalupe Hidalgo; gold is discovered at Sutter's Mill in Coloma

1849—Steamer *California* brings the first Gold Rush passengers (365) to San Francisco; citizens set up state government, without waiting for Congressional action; state constitution provides for a public-school system

1850—California becomes the thirty-first state on September 9

1854—Sacramento designated as the state capital

1861—Completion of the first transcontinental telegraph line signals the end of the Pony Express

1869—The first transcontinental railroad system is completed, linking Sacramento with the eastern United States

1873—Modoc War, California's last Indian War

1879—Second state constitution is adopted

1890—Yosemite National Park is established

1892—Conservation group, the Sierra Club, is founded by John Muir

1905-1907—Floodwaters from the Colorado River form the 450-square-mile (1,165-square-kilometer) Salton Sea in southeastern California

1906 — San Francisco's great earthquake and fire kills seven hundred people, leaves three hundred thousand more homeless, and destroys more than twenty-eight thousand buildings

1907 — First commercial film made in California, *The Count of Monte Cristo*, is completed near Los Angeles

1914 — Panama Canal is completed, shortening the sea route between California and the eastern United States

1932 — Los Angeles hosts the Olympic Games at the Coliseum

1935 — First phase of the federal government's Central Valley Project to bring water to the Central California Valley begins

1936 — Hoover Dam is completed, providing irrigation water, power, and flood control in southern California and neighboring states

1937 — Golden Gate Bridge across San Francisco Bay is completed

1940 — California's first major freeway, the Arroyo Serro, between Los Angeles and Pasadena is completed (now called the Pasadena Freeway)

1942 — President Roosevelt orders internment of California's Japanese Americans during World War II

1945 — United Nations is founded at the San Francisco Conference

1953 — Governor Earl Warren resigns to become chief justice of the United States Supreme Court; Californian Richard M. Nixon takes office as vice-president of the United States, under Dwight D. Eisenhower

1960 — California Water Project initiated; Winter Olympics held at Squaw Valley

1965 — Thirty-four people die as racial riots break out in the Watts section of Los Angeles; Cesar Chavez's National Farm Workers Association wins its first strike

1968 — Richard Nixon elected president of the United States; re-elected 1972

1971 — Earthquake in Los Angeles area kills sixty-four people and causes more than $500 million in damage

1973 — Tom Bradley elected to first of four terms as mayor of Los Angeles; first black mayor of a major American city

1974 — Richard Nixon resigns as president during Watergate scandal

1976 — BART (the Bay Area Rapid Transit system) opens, connecting San Francisco, Alameda, and Contra Costa counties

1977—Rose Elizabeth Bird, first woman chief justice of California's supreme court, takes office

1978—California voters approve Proposition 13, cutting local property taxes by 57 percent

1980—Ronald Reagan elected president of the United States

1984—San Francisco hosts Democratic National Convention; Los Angeles hosts the summer Olympic Games for the second time in the twentieth century

1986—State lottery becomes official and its income is used to support state schools

1987—Earthquake in Los Angeles area kills three and causes nearly $360 million in property damage

1988—Pope John Paul II beatifies Franciscan priest Junípero Serra, the Spanish missionary who founded nine missions in California

1989—A devastating earthquake measuring 6.9 on the Richter Scale hits the San Francisco-Oakland area, causing sixty-two deaths and nearly $6 billion in damage

IMPORTANT PEOPLE

ANSEL ADAMS

AMBROSE BIERCE

Ansel Adams (1902-1984), born in San Francisco; photographer and conservationist; noted for dramatic pictures of western landscapes and for sharply focused, finely detailed pictures of small objects of nature; helped found departments of photography at the New York Museum of Modern Art in 1940 and at the California School of Fine Art (now the San Francisco Art Institute) in 1946

Luis Walter Alvarez (1911-1988), born in San Francisco; physicist and educator; professor at University of California, Berkeley (1938-88); winner of 1966 Nobel Prize in physics; noted for his studies of atomic nuclei and subatomic particles

Gertrude Franklin Atherton (1857-1948), born in San Francisco; novelist; best known for *Before the Gringo Came* (1894), *The Californians* (1898), and *Black Oxen* (1923)

Mary Hunter Austin (1868-1934); novelist and playwright; wrote sympathetically of the Indians of California and the southwest in *The Land of Little Rain* and *The Arrow-Maker*

Ambrose Gwinett Bierce (1842-1914); author and journalist; lived and worked in San Francisco from 1866 to 1897; best known for Civil War stories in *Tales of Soldiers and Civilians* (1891) and *The Cynic's Word Book* (1906, later known as *The Devil's Dictionary*)

Albert Bierstadt (1830-1902); landscape artist; traveled the American West beginning in the 1850s and became known for his romantic mountain scenes and his historic paintings

Thomas Bradley (1917-   ); lawyer and public official; member of Los Angeles police force (1940-61); first black mayor of Los Angeles; the only person ever elected mayor of Los Angeles four times (1973, 1977, 1981, 1985)

THOMAS BRADLEY

Edmund Gerald (Pat) Brown (1905-   ), born in San Francisco; politician; district attorney, San Francisco (1943-50); attorney general, California (1950-59); governor of California (1959-67)

Edmund Gerald (Jerry) Brown, Jr. (1938-   ), born in San Francisco; politician; secretary of state, California (1971-1974); governor of California (1975-83)

Luther Burbank (1849-1926); plant breeder and horticulturist; settled in California in 1875; developed more than 220 new varieties of flowers, fruits, and grains and more than 40 varieties of plums

Christopher (Kit) Carson (1809-1868); frontiersman; guided John Frémont's exploration parties in the 1840s; when war broke out with Mexico in 1846, Frémont, Carson, and the others joined the American settlers in California in a revolt against Mexican authorities there

LUTHER BURBANK

Owen Chamberlain (1920-   ), born in San Francisco; physicist; joined the University of California faculty in 1948 and became a professor in 1958; shared the 1959 Nobel Prize in physics

Raymond Thornton Chandler (1888-1959); novelist; created detective Philip Marlowe; six Marlowe novels became movies, including *The Big Sleep* (1946) and *The Long Goodbye* (1953)

Charles Spencer (Charlie) Chaplin (1889-1977); pioneer Hollywood silent film actor and director; created the silent film character "the Tramp"; known for his films *Modern Times* (1936) and *The Great Dictator* (1940); received an honorary Academy Award in 1972 for his contributions to the film industry

CHARLIE CHAPLIN

Cesar Estrada Chavez (1927-   ); labor-union organizer and spokesman for California's Mexican-American farm workers; in 1962 organized California grape pickers into a union that in 1973 became the United Farm Workers of America; to win collective bargaining rights for the union, led nationwide boycotts against the purchase of California-grown table grapes and lettuce

James John (Gentleman Jim) Corbett (1866-1933), born in San Francisco; world heavyweight boxing champion (1892-97); considered one of the first "scientific" boxers

Alan Macgregor Cranston (1914-   ), born in Palo Alto; political leader; in 1953 helped found the California Democratic Council; state controller (1959-67); U.S. senator (1969-   )

CESAR CHAVEZ

WALT DISNEY

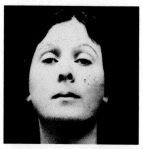

ISADORA DUNCAN

DIANNE FEINSTEIN

JOHN FRÉMONT

Cecil Blount De Mille (1881-1959); pioneer motion-picture producer and director; started in Hollywood with silent films in 1913; went on to produce spectacular large-cast Biblical films; won the 1952 Academy Award for best picture of the year with *The Greatest Show on Earth*

George Deukmejian, Jr. (1928-   ); lawyer and public official; member of the California assembly (1963-67); member of the state senate (1967-79); state attorney general (1978); governor of California (1983-   )

Joan Didion (1934-   ), born in Sacramento; essayist and novelist; uses California culture, locale, and people as themes

Walter Elias (Walt) Disney (1901-1966); pioneer motion-picture animator and producer; created the cartoon character Mickey Mouse in 1928 and produced the first film in full color in 1932; created Disneyland amusement park in California and Disney World in Florida

Donald Wills Douglas (1892-1981); aircraft manufacturer; formed the Douglas Company in Santa Monica (1920-21), which later became the McDonnell Douglas Corporation

Isadora Duncan (1878-1927), born in San Francisco; dancer; created "interpretative dancing"

Clinton (Clint) Eastwood, Jr. (1930-   ), born in San Francisco; actor and director; noted for portraying strong, silent heroes of the West and as the antiestablishment police officer *Dirty Harry* (1971); mayor of Carmel-by-the-Sea (1986-   )

March Kong Fong Eu (1927-   ), born in Oakdale; public official; member of the California assembly (1966-74); California secretary of state (1975-   )

Dianne Feinstein (1933-   ), born in San Francisco; public official; became mayor of San Francisco in 1978 when she succeeded assassinated Mayor George R. Moscone; was reelected mayor in 1979 and 1983

Lawrence Ferlinghetti (1919-   ); poet; influenced "beat poetry" of the 1950s; owner of City Lights, a San Francisco bookstore and publishing company that sells and publishes the works of experimental writers

John Charles Frémont (1813-1890); explorer and public official; explored much of the area between the Rocky Mountains and the Pacific Ocean; helped bring California into the Union; one of the state's first two senators (1850-51)

John William Gardner (1912-   ), born in Los Angeles; public official; president of the Carnegie Corporation of New York (1955-65); secretary of health, education and welfare under President L.B. Johnson (1965-68); founder and first president of Common Cause, a group that promotes urban and social legislation and government reform (1970-77)

Judy Garland (1922-1969); born Frances Gumm; actress and singer; appeared in her first film at the age of fourteen; best known for her role as Dorothy in *The Wizard of Oz*

David Lewelyn Wark (D. W.) Griffith (1875-1948); pioneer motion-picture director and producer; turned film making into an art with his editing techniques; best known for *The Birth of a Nation* (1915), a historical film about the Civil War and the rise of the Ku Klux Klan

George Ellery Hale (1868-1938); astronomer; founded and directed Wisconsin's Yerkes Observatory (1895-1905) and California's Mount Wilson Observatory (1904-23); planned the construction of the Hale Reflecting Telescope at the Palomar Observatory near San Diego

Francis Brett (Bret) Harte (1836-1902); author; wrote stories of the 1849 California Gold Rush; edited *The Overland Monthly* (1868-71), a San Francisco magazine in which he published his best known short stories, "The Luck of Roaring Camp" (1868) and "The Outcasts of Poker Flat" (1869)

Samuel Ichiye (S.I.) Hayakawa (1906-   ); educator and public official; taught at San Francisco State College (1955-58) and became its president (1968-73); took a strong stand to end the turbulent student protests of the late 1960s; U.S. senator from California (1977-83); noted for his works on semantics

William Randolph Hearst (1863-1951), born in San Francisco; journalist and publisher; to attract readers, he developed "yellow journalism," which emphasizes sensationalism over truth in news reporting; publisher of the *San Francisco Examiner* (1885); by 1937 owned twenty-five dailies and several magazines; his California estate at San Simeon is now a state park

Collis Potter Huntington (1821-1900); Sacramento-based merchant and financier; helped finance the Central Pacific and its linkup with the Union Pacific in 1869; president of the Southern Pacific (Railroad) Company

Helen Hunt Jackson (1830-1885); novelist, poet, and social reformer; wrote of the U.S. government's shameful mismanagement of Indian affairs in *A Century of Dishonor* (1881) and the mistreatment of Indians in the novel *Ramona* (1884)

(John) Robinson Jeffers (1887-1962); narrative poet; in 1914 settled on the north coast of California; noted for *Tamar* (1924), *Roan Stallion* (1925), and later collections of poetry

Joseph Frank (Buster) Keaton (1895-1966); child vaudeville star and popular silent film comedian; motion pictures included *The General* (1927) and *The Navigator* (1924)

Jean-Louis Lebris de (Jack) Kerouac (1922-1969); author; a leader of the 1950s and 1960s "beat" movement of young people; best known for his novel *On The Road* (1957)

JUDY GARLAND

S.I. HAYAKAWA

WM. RANDOLPH HEARST

JACK KEROUAC

JACK LONDON

AIMEE SEMPLE McPHERSON

MARILYN MONROE

JOHN MUIR

Dorothea Lange (1895-1965); photographer; settled in San Francisco; recorded California life in pictures of migratory farm workers of the 1930s, Mormon towns, and the Japanese Americans who were removed to relocation camps during World War II

Ernest Orlando Lawrence (1901-1958); physicist; member of the University of California Berkeley faculty (1928-58) and director of radiation laboratory (1936-58); invented the cyclotron, a machine that accelerates atomic particles; won the 1939 Nobel Prize in physics and the 1957 Enrico Fermi Award

John Griffith (Jack) London (1876-1916), born in San Francisco; novelist and short-story writer; among his most-famous works are the collection of tales of the 1897 Klondike gold rush called *The Son of the Wolf* (1900) and his novel *The Call of the Wild* (1903); his California home near Santa Rosa is now a state historical park

Charles Fletcher Lummis (1859-1928); writer and explorer; learned Indian languages and customs; became an expert on the history and archaeology of the Southwest; founded the Southwest Museum of Los Angeles

Ross MacDonald (1915-1983), born Kenneth Millar in Los Gatos; author of detective novels; created the character Lew Archer, a private detective whose exploits take place in southern California

Edwin Mattison McMillan (1907-   ); born in Redondo Beach; scientist; associate director of the University of California, Berkeley, radiation laboratory (1954-58); shared the 1952 Nobel Prize in chemistry; won the 1963 Atoms for Peace Award

Aimee Semple McPherson (1890-1944); evangelist; conducted revival meetings throughout the United States; preached on an evangelist radio station; founded the International Church of the Foursquare Gospel (1927)

Marilyn Monroe (1926-1962), born Norma Jean Baker or Norma Jean Mortenson in Los Angeles; actress and world-famous symbol of Hollywood sex and glamor; starred in some thirty films

John Muir (1838-1914); explorer, naturalist, and writer; campaigned for U.S. forest conservation; convinced President Theodore Roosevelt to set aside millions of acres of national forest reserves, the first of the kind; founded the Sierra Club, a major conservation organization; helped establish Yosemite and Sequoia national parks (1890)

Richard Milhous Nixon (1913-   ), born in Yorba Linda; thirty-seventh president of the United States; U.S. congressman (1946-50); U.S. senator (1950-52); vice-president of the United States (1952-60); only native-born Californian ever to serve as president (1969-74); only president ever to resign from the office (August 9, 1974, during the Watergate Scandal)

George Smith Patton, Jr. (1885-1945), born in San Gabriel; career army officer; West Point Military Academy graduate (1909); commanded tank corps in World Wars I and II in Europe

Linus Carl Pauling (1901-   ); chemist; taught at California Institute of Technology (1931-63), University of California, San Diego (1968-69), and Stanford University (1969-   ); received the 1954 Nobel Prize for chemistry and the 1962 Nobel Prize for peace

Ronald Wilson Reagan (1911-   ), fortieth president of the United States; motion-picture actor who appeared in more than fifty films; governor of California (1967-75); president (1981-89)

William Saroyan (1908-1981), born in Fresno; author and playwright; won the 1940 Pulitzer Prize in drama for his play *The Time of Your Life*

Glenn Theodore Seaborg (1912-   ); scientist; chancellor at University of California, Berkeley (1958-61); chairman of the U.S. Atomic Energy Commission (1961-71); shared the 1951 Nobel Prize in chemistry; won the 1959 Enrico Fermi Award

David Oliver Selznick (1902-1965); motion-picture producer; directed Selznick International Pictures Inc. in Hollywood (1935-40); won Academy Awards for *Gone With the Wind* (1939) and *Rebecca* (1940)

Junípero (Miguel José) Serra (1713-1784); Franciscan missionary; founded a number of missions that have become present-day settlements in California

Leland Stanford (1824-1893); railroad magnate and public official; governor of California (1862-63); U.S. senator (1885-93); developed and served as president of both the Central Pacific and Southern railroads; founded Stanford University (1885)

John Ernest Steinbeck (1902-1968), born in Salinas; novelist; best known for *The Grapes of Wrath*, the 1940 Pulitzer Prizewinning story of poor Oklahoma farmers who migrated to California during the 1930s depression; received the 1962 Nobel Prize for lifetime achievement in literature

Levi Strauss (1829-1902); clothing manufacturer; opened a wholesale business in San Francisco (1853); in 1874 began producing the famous blue denim jeans reinforced with rivets

John Augustus Sutter (1803-1880); California pioneer; received a land grant from the Mexican government (1839) on which he founded what now is Sacramento; the 1848 gold strike at his sawmill led to the California gold rush of 1849

Shirley Temple (Black) (1928-   ), born in Santa Monica; actress and public official; starred in more than twenty-five musical films; U.S. representative to the U.N. General Assembly (1969-70); ambassador to Ghana (1974-76); first woman chief of protocol in the U.S. Department of State (1976-77)

GEORGE S. PATTON

RONALD REAGAN

LEVI STRAUSS

SHIRLEY TEMPLE

EARL WARREN

JOHN WAYNE

Mariano Guadalupe Vallejo (1808-1890); California pioneer; built the Sonoma garrison on the northern frontier; commanded California troops (1838) under Mexican rule; member of the California state constitutional convention (1849); member of first state senate (1850)

Earl Warren (1891-1974), born in Los Angeles; jurist; attorney general of California (1939-43); governor (1943-53); chief justice of U.S. Supreme Court (1953-69); noted for writing the opinion in the 1954 ruling that outlawed racial segregation in public schools; chaired the 1964 presidential committee to investigate the assassination of President Kennedy

John Wayne (1907-1979), born Marion Michael Morrison; motion-picture actor; famous for "he-man" roles, especially in the western films *Stagecoach* (1939), *Red River* (1948), and his Academy-Award-winning performance in *True Grit* (1969)

Caspar Willard Weinberger (1917-   ), born in San Francisco; lawyer and public official; member of California assembly (1952-58); state finance director (1968-69); chairman of the Federal Trade Commission (1970); director of the Office of Management and Budget (1970-72); secretary of health, education and welfare (1973-75); secretary of defense (1981-87)

Edward Weston (1886-1958); photographer; noted for dramatic, sharply focused portraits, California seascapes and landscapes, and closeups of nature; first photographer to win a Guggenheim Fellowship, an award given to scholars, artists, and scientists

GOVERNORS

Peter H. Burnett	1849-1851	Henry T. Gage	1899-1903
John McDougal	1851-1852	George C. Pardee	1903-1907
John Bigler	1852-1856	James N. Gillett	1907-1911
John Neely Johnson	1856-1858	Hiram W. Johnson	1911-1917
John B. Weller	1858-1860	William D. Stephens	1917-1923
Milton S. Latham	1860	Friend William Richard	1923-1927
John G. Downey	1860-1862	Clement C. Young	1927-1931
Leland Stanford	1862-1863	James Rolph, Jr.	1931-1934
Frederick F. Low	1863-1867	Frank F. Merriam	1934-1939
Henry H. Haight	1867-1871	Culbert L. Olson	1939-1943
Newton Booth	1871-1875	Earl Warren	1943-1953
Romualdo Pacheco	1875	Goodwin J. Knight	1953-1959
William Irwin	1875-1880	Edmund G. Brown	1959-1967
George C. Perkins	1880-1883	Ronald Reagan	1967-1975
George Stoneman	1883-1887	Edmund G. Brown, Jr.	1975-1983
Washington Bartlett	1887	George Deukmejian	1983-
Robert W. Waterman	1887-1891		
Henry H. Markham	1891-1895		
James H. Budd	1895-1899		

RL 86-S-6

Topography

| 0 | 200 | 400 MI. |
| 0 | 200 | 400 KM. |

| 5,000 m. | 2,000 m. | 1,000 m. | 500 m. | 200 m. | 100 m. | Sea |
| 16,404 ft. | 6,562 ft. | 3,281 ft. | 1,640 ft. | 656 ft. | 328 ft. | Level Below |

MAP KEY

Place	Grid
Alameda	h8
Alameda Naval Air Station	h8
Alhambra	m12
Altadena	m12
Amargosa Range (mountain range)	D5
American (river)	C3
Anaheim	F5;n13
Antioch	h9
Apple Valley	E5
Arcadia	m12
Arcata	B1
Arroyo Grande	E3
Atascadero	E3
Atwater	D3
Azusa	m13
Bakersfield	E4
Banning	F5
Barstow	E5
Beale Air Force Base	C3
Bellflower	n12
Belmont	h8
Benicia	C2;g8
Berkeley	D2;h8
Beverly Hills	m12
Big Sur	D3
Big Pine Mountain (mountain)	E4
Black Butte Lake (lake)	C2
Bodega Head (head)	C2
Brawley	F6
Brea	n13
Buena Park	n12
Burbank	E4;m12
Burlingame	h8
Cabrillo National Monument	o15
Cache Creek (creek)	C2
Calexico	F6
California Aqueduct (aqueduct)	E4,5
Camp Pendelton Marine Corps Base	F5
Campbell	k9
Capitan Reservoir (reservoir)	o16
Carlsbad	F5
Carpinteria	E4
Cascade Range (mountain range)	B2,3
Castle Air Force Base	D3
Castro Valley	h8
Cedar Mountain (mountain)	B3
Ceres	D3
Chanchelulla Peak (mountain)	B2
Channel Islands National Monument	E4
Channel Islands National Park	F4
Chatsworth Reservoir (reservoir)	m11
Chemehuevi Indian Reservation	E6
Chico	C3
Chino	E5;m13
Chocolate Mountains (mountains)	F6
Chula Vista	F5;o15
Clair Engle Lake (lake)	B2
Claremont	m13
Claremont (mountain)	C3
Clear Lake (lake)	C2
Clear Lake Reservoir (reservoir)	B3
Clovis	D4
Coachella Canal (canal)	F6
Coast Ranges (mountain ranges)	B,C2;D,E3,4
Colorado (river)	E,F6
Colorado River Aqueduct (aqueduct)	E,F6
Colorado River Indian Reservation	E,F6
Compton	n12
Concord	h8
Corona	F5;n13
Coronado	F5;o15
Costa Mesa	n13
Covina	m13
Culver City	m12
Cuyama	E3,4
Cuyamaca Peak (mountain)	F5
Daly City	h8
Danville	h9
Davis	C3
Death Valley	D5
Death Valley National Monument	D,E5
Devils Postpile National Monument	D4
Diablo (mountain range)	D3;h,k9,10
Donner Pass (mountain pass)	C3
Downey	n12
Eagle Lake (lake)	B3
Eagle Peak (mountain)	B3
East Los Angeles	m12
Edwards Air Force Base	E5
Eel (river)	B1,2
El Cajon	F5;o15
El Capitan Reservoir (reservoir)	o16
El Centro	F6
El Cerrito	h8
El Toro Marine Corps. Base	n13
Elk Grove	C3
Encinitas	F5
Estero Bay (bay)	E3
Eureka	B1
Excelsior Mountain (mountain)	C4
Eylar Mountain (mountain)	D3;k9
Fairfield	C2
Fallbrook	F5
Feather (river)	C3
Feather Falls	C3
Folsom	C3
Fontana	m14
Fort Bidwell Indian Reservation	B3,4
Fort Bragg	C2
Fort Mohave Indian Reservation	E6
Fort Ord	D3
Fort Yuma Indian Reservation	F6
Fountain Peak (mountain)	E6
Freel Peak (mountain)	C4
Fremont	D2;h9
Fresno	D4
Fullerton	n13
Garden Grove	n13
Gardena	n12
George Air Force Base	E5
Gilroy	D3
Glendale	m12
Glendora	m13
Golden Gate Bridge (bridge)	h7
Golden Gate National Recreation Area	h7
Goose Lake (lake)	B3
Gulf of Santa Cataline (gulf)	F5
Hanford	D4
Hawthorne	n12
Hayward	h8
Hemet	F5
Hesperia	E5
Highland Peak (mountain)	C4
Hollister	D3
Honey Lake (lake)	B3
Hoopa Valley Indian Reservation	B2
Hot Springs Peak (mountain)	B3
Huntington Beach	F5;n13
Imperial Beach	o15
Indio	F5
Inglewood	n12
Iron Gate Reservoir (reservoir)	B2
Irvine	n13
John Muir National Historic Site	h8
Joshua Tree National Monument	F5,6
Junipero Serra Peak (mountain)	D3
Kern (river)	D,E4
King Peak (mountain)	B1
Kings (river)	D4
Kings Canyon National Park	D4
Klamath (river)	B1,2
Klamath Mountains (mountains)	B2
La Canada	m12
La Habra	n13
La Mesa	F5;o15
La Verne	m13
Laguna Beach	F5;n13
Lake Almanor (lake)	B3
Lake Berryessa (reservoir)	C2
Lake Crowley (Lake)	D4
Lake Mathews (lake)	n14
Lake Oroville (lake)	C3
Lake Success (lake)	D4
Lake Tahoe (lake)	C3
Lakeside	F5;o16
Lakewood	n12
Lancaster	E4
Larkspur	h7
Lassen Peak (volcano)	B2,3
Lassen Volcanic National Park	B3
Lava Beds National Monument	B3
Lemon Grove	o15
Lemoore Naval Air Station	D4
Livermore	h9
Lodi	C3
Lompoc	E3
Long Beach	F4;n12
Long Beach Naval Shipyard	n12
Los Altos	k8
Los Angeles	E4;m12
Los Angeles Aqueduct (aqueduct)	E4,5
Los Banos	D3
Los Gatos	D2,3
Lower Otay Reservoir (reservoir)	o16
Lowest Point in the United States	D5
Lynwood	n12
Mad (river)	B1,2
Madera	D3
Manhattan Beach	n12
Manteca	D3
March Air Force Base	F5
Martinez	C,D2;g8
Mather Air Force Base	C3
McClellan Air Force Base	C3
McKittrick Summit (mountain)	E4
Menlo Park	k8
Merced	D3
Merced (river)	D3
Mill Valley	D2;h7
Millbrae	h8
Miramar Naval Air Station	F5;o15
Mission Indian Reservations	F5
Mission Viejo	n13
Modesto	D3
Moffett Field Naval Air Station	k8
Mojave (river)	E5
Mojave Desert (desert)	E5
Mokelumne (river)	C3
Mono Lake (lake)	C,D4
Monrovia	m12,13
Montclair	m13
Montebello	m12
Monterey	D3
Monterey Bay (bay))	D2,3
Monterey Park	m12
Morgan Hill	D3
Mountain View	k8
Mount Bidwell (mountain)	B3
Mount Diablo (mountain)	h9
Mount Hamilton (mountain)	k9
Mount Humphreys (mountain)	D4
Mount Inyo (mountain)	D5
Mount Lola (mountain)	C3
Mount Pinos (mountain)	E4
Mount Ritter (mountain)	D4
Mount Shasta (volcano)	B2
Mount Tamalpais (mountain)	h7
Mount Whitney (mountain)	D4
Mount Wilson (mountain)	m12
Muir Woods National Monument	h7
Nacimiento Reservoir (reservoir)	E3
Napa	C2
National City	F5;o15
Newark	h8
Newhall	E4
Newport Beach	n13
North Island Naval Air Station	o15
North Palisade (mountain)	D4
Norton Air Force Base	E5
Norwalk	n12
Novato	C2
Oakland	D2;h8
Oceanside	F5
Oildale	E4
Olancha Peak (mountain)	D4
Ontario	E4;m13
Orange	n13
Outer Santa Barbara Passage	F4,5
Owens (river)	D4
Owens Lake (lake)	D5
Oxnard	E4
Pacific Grove	D3
Pacific Ocean	B1;C1,2;D2,3;E2,3,4;F3,4,5; h,k7;m11,n11,12,13;o,p15
Pacifica	h8
Palm Springs	F5
Palmdale	E4
Palo Alto	D2;k8
Palomar Mountain (mountain)	F5
Palos Verdes Estates	n12
Panamint Range (mountain range)	D5
Paradise	C3
Pasadena	E4;m12
Petaluma	C2
Pico Rivera	n12
Piedmont	h8
Pillar Point (point)	k8
Pinnacles National Monument	D3
Pinole	g,h8
Pit (river)	B3
Pittsburg	g9
Piute Peak (mountain)	E4
Pleasant Hill	h8
Pleasanton	h9
Point Arena (point)	C2
Point Conception (point)	E3
Point La Jolla (point)	o15
Point Mugu Naval Air Station	E4
Point Piedras Blancas (point)	E3
Point Pinos (point)	D3
Point Reyes (point)	C,D2
Point Reyes National Seashore	C2
Point Sal (point)	E3
Point San Luis (point)	E3
Point Sur (point)	D3
Point Vincente (point)	n12
Pomona	E5;m13
Porterville	D4
Port Hueneme	E4
Poway	F5
Prado Flood Control Basin	n13
Red Mountain (mountain)	B2
Redding	B2
Redlands	E5
Redondo Beach	n12
Redwood City	D2;k8
Redwood National Park	B2
Reedley	D4
Rialto	m14
Richmond	D2;h8
Ridgecrest	E5
Riverside	F5;n14
Roseville	C3
Round Valley Indian Reservation	C2
Rubidoux	n14
Russian (river)	C2
Sacramento	C3
Sacramento (river)	C3
Sacramento Valley (valley)	B,C2,3
Salinas	D3
Salinas (river)	B2
Salmon Mountains (mountains)	C2
Salt Point (point)	F5,6
Salton Sea	F5,6
San Anselmo	h7
San Benito Mountain (mountain)	D3
San Bernardino	E5;m14
San Bruno	D2;h8
San Carlos	h,k8
San Clemente	F5
San Clemente Island (island)	F4
San Diego	F5;o14
San Diego (river)	o15,16
San Diego Naval Station	o15
San Diego Naval Training Center	o15
San Fernando	m12
San Francisco	D2;h8
San Francisco Bay (bay)	h8
San Gabriel	m12
San Gabriel Mountains (mountains)	m12,13
San Gorgonio Mountain (mountain)	E5
San Jacinto Peak (mountain)	F5
San Joaquin (river)	D,E3,4
San Joaquin (valley)	D3, k9
San Jose	D3
San Juan Capistrano	F5
San Leandro	h8
San Luis Obispo	E3
San Marino	m12
San Mateo	D2;h8
San Miguel Island (island)	E3
San Nicolas Island (island)	F4
San Pablo Bay (bay)	g8
San Pedro Channel (channel)	n12
San Rafael	D2;h7
San Rafael Mountains (mountains)	E3,4
San Vicente Reservoir (reservoir)	o16
Sanger	D4
Santa Ana	F5;n13
Santa Ana (river)	n13
Santa Ana Mountains (mountains)	n13
Santa Barbara	E4
Santa Barbara Channel (channel)	E3,4
Santa Catalina Island (island)	F4
Santa Clara	D2;k9
Santa Clara (river)	E4
Santa Cruz	D2
Santa Cruz Island (island)	E,F4
Santa Lucia (mountain range)	D,E3
Santa Maria	E3
Santa Monica	m12
Santa Paula	E4
Santa Rosa	C2
Santa Rosa Island (island)	E,F3,4
Santee	o16
Santiago Peak (mountain)	n14
Santiago Reservoir (reservoir)	n13
Saratoga	k8
Searles Lake (lake)	E5
Selma	D4
Sequoia National Park	D4
Shasta Lake (lake)	B2
Sierra Madre	m12
Sierra Nevada (mountains)	C,D,E3,4
Simi Valley	E4;m11
Siskiyou Mountains (mountains)	B2
South Gate	n12
South Lake Tahoe	C4
South San Francisco	h8
South Ventana Cone (mountain)	D3
Spring Valley	o16
Stockton	D3,h10
Sunnyvale	k8
Tehachapi Mountains (mountains)	E4
Telescope Peak (mountain)	D5
Thompson Peak (mountain)	B2
Toro Peak (mountain)	F5
Torrance	n12
Tracy	D3;h10
Travis Air Force Base	C2
Treasure Island Naval Station	h8
Trinidad Head (head)	B1
Trinity (river)	B2
Trinity River, South Fork	B2
Trinity Center	B2
Trinity Mountains (mountains)	B2
Tulare	D4
Tule River Indian Reservation	D4
Tuolumne (river)	D3
Turlock	D3
Twentynine Palms Marine Corps Base	E5
Ukiah	C2
Union City	h8
Upland	E5;m13
Vacaville	C3
Vallejo	C2
Vandenberg Air Force Base	E3
Ventura	E4
Victorville	E5
Visalia	D4
Vista	F5
Walnut Creek	h8
Warner Mountains (mountains)	A,B3
Watsonville	D3
West Covina	m13
Westminster	n12
Wheeler Peak (mountain)	C4
Whiskeytown-Shasta-Trinity National Recreation Area	B2,3
White Mountain Peak (mountain)	D4
White Mountains (mountains)	D4
Whittier	F4;m,n12
Woodland	C3
Yosemite National Park	C,D4
Yuba (river)	C3
Yuba City	C3

© Copyright by RAND McNALLY & COMPANY, R.L. 87-S-127

OREGON

NEVADA

Pacific Ocean

MEXICO

San Francisco
Oakland
San Jose
Sacramento
Fresno
Los Angeles
Long Beach
San Diego
Bakersfield
Stockton
Modesto
Eureka
Redding
Santa Rosa
San Rafael
Vallejo
Berkeley
Monterey
Santa Cruz
Salinas
San Luis Obispo
Santa Barbara
Ventura
Santa Maria
Lancaster
Palmdale
San Bernardino
Riverside
Santa Ana
Anaheim
Newport Beach
Oceanside
Escondido
National City
Chula Vista
Tijuana
Mexicali
Yuma

Klamath Falls
Lakeview
Las Vegas
Henderson
Boulder City
Hoover Dam

DEATH VALLEY NAT. MON.
YOSEMITE NATIONAL PARK
SEQUOIA NAT. PARK
KINGS CANYON NAT. PARK
JOSHUA TREE NAT. MON.
MOJAVE DESERT
COLORADO DESERT
IMPERIAL VALLEY
CHANNEL ISLANDS NAT. PARK

MT. WHITNEY 14,494
MT. SHASTA (VOL.) 14,162

San Francisco area inset:
San Rafael, San Anselmo, Larkspur, Sausalito, Daly City, Pacifica, Millbrae, Burlingame, San Mateo, Belmont, San Carlos, Redwood City, Menlo Park, Palo Alto, Mountain View, Sunnyvale, Santa Clara, San Jose, Campbell, Los Altos, Half Moon Bay, Oakland, Alameda, San Leandro, Hayward, Fremont, Newark, Berkeley, El Cerrito, Richmond, Pinole, Martinez, Concord, Walnut Creek, Pleasant Hill, Danville, Livermore, Pleasanton, Stockton, Antioch, Pittsburg, Benicia, Crockett

Los Angeles area inset:
San Fernando, Burbank, Glendale, Pasadena, Altadena, Sierra Madre, Arcadia, Monrovia, Azusa, Glendora, Upland, Montclair, Claremont, Ontario, San Bernardino, Rialto, Fontana, Beverly Hills, Santa Monica, Culver City, Inglewood, Hawthorne, Manhattan Beach, Redondo Beach, Torrance, Alhambra, San Gabriel, Monterey Park, Montebello, South Gate, Downey, Whittier, La Habra, Brea, Fullerton, Corona, Riverside, Pomona, W. Covina, Covina, Compton, Lynwood, Bellflower, Norwalk, Buena Park, Anaheim, Orange, Santa Ana, Garden Grove, Westminster, Costa Mesa, Newport Beach, Huntington Beach, Long Beach, Lakewood, Palos Verdes Estates

San Diego area inset:
Del Mar, La Jolla, San Diego, La Mesa, El Cajon, Santee, Lakeside, Lemon Grove, National City, Lincoln Acres, Chula Vista, Imperial Beach, Coronado, Tijuana, MEXICO

Statute Miles
Kilometers
Lambert Conformal Conic Projection

B-520505-21—6—12"
COSMO SERIES CALIFORNIA
Copyright by RAND McNALLY & COMPANY
Made in U.S.A.
Longitude West of Greenwich

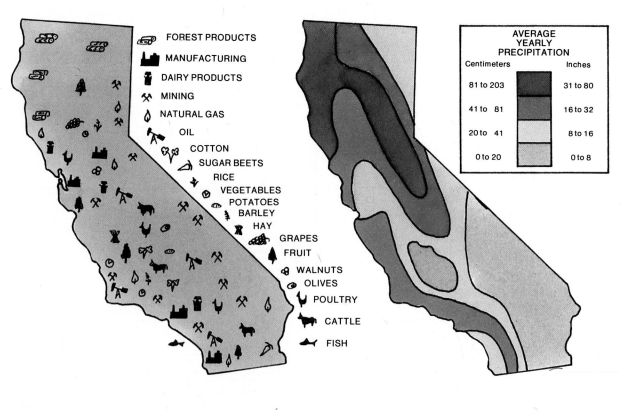

FOREST PRODUCTS
MANUFACTURING
DAIRY PRODUCTS
MINING
NATURAL GAS
OIL
COTTON
SUGAR BEETS
RICE
VEGETABLES
POTATOES
BARLEY
HAY
GRAPES
FRUIT
WALNUTS
OLIVES
POULTRY
CATTLE
FISH

AVERAGE
YEARLY
PRECIPITATION

Centimeters		Inches
81 to 203		31 to 80
41 to 81		16 to 32
20 to 41		8 to 16
0 to 20		0 to 8

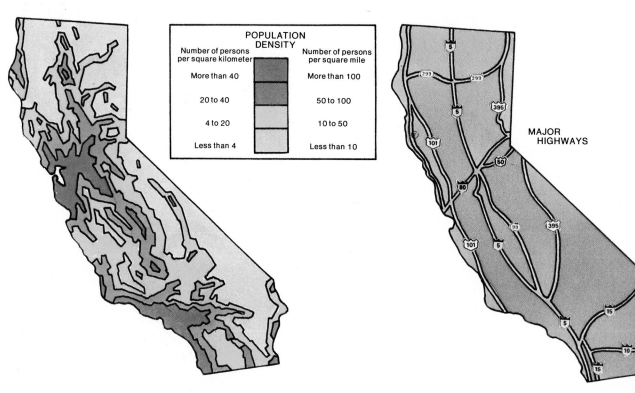

POPULATION
DENSITY

Number of persons per square kilometer		Number of persons per square mile
More than 40		More than 100
20 to 40		50 to 100
4 to 20		10 to 50
Less than 4		Less than 10

MAJOR
HIGHWAYS

TOPOGRAPHY

Courtesy of Hammond, Incorporated

Maplewood, New Jersey

COUNTIES

An unusual cloud formation reflects a breathtaking Death Valley sunset.

INDEX

Page numbers that appear in boldface type indicate illustrations

Abdul-Jabbar, Kareem, 88
Adams, Ansel, 83, 126, **126**
agriculture, 35, 56, 71-74, 96, 103, 117
air pollution, 63, **63**
airports, 77
Alameda, 60
Alcatraz Island, 120
Alexander Valley, 96

All American Canal, 73
Alvarez, Luis Walter, 126
American River, 13, 42
Anaheim, 26, 106, 107
animal, state, 109
animals, 16, 31, 104, 115
Anza, Juan Bautista de, 33
aqueducts, 15, 73
architecture, 84

area, 12, 112
Arizona, 12
Armour, Philip, 46
Asians, in California, 24, 25, 27, 50-51, 59, 65, 85
Atherton, Gertrude Franklin, 126
Austin, Mary Hunter, 81, 126
aviation industry, 59

Badwater, 11
Bakersfield, 103
Balboa Beach, **5**, 106
Balboa Park, 107, **119**
Bank of America, 56
Bay Area Rapid Transit (BART), 77
beaches, 7, **12**, 106
Bear Flag Revolt, 39
Belmont, 98
Bidwell-Bartleson Party, 38
Bierce, Ambrose, 80, 126, **126**
Bierstadt, Albert, 83, 127
Big Sur, 102, **102**, 122
Bird, Rose, 64
bird, state, **108**, 109
birds, 16, 115
blacks, 24, 60, 61-62
Boco, 15
borders of state, 12, 111
Bradbury, Ray, 82
Bradley, Thomas, 64, 127, **127**
Bradley Building, 105
Bridalveil Falls, **18**
bridges, 77
bristlecone pine, 16
British, in California, 32, **32**, 38
Brown, Jerry, 64, 127
Brown, Pat, 63, 64, 127
Brown, Willie, 64
Burbank, Luther, 127, **127**
business and trade, 7, 117-118
cable car, **4**
Cabrillo, Juan Rodriguez, 31
Cabrillo National Monument, 120
California, origin of name, 36, 109
California State University, 72
California Water Project, 73
Californios, 36-37
Cannery Row, 81
capitals, state, 47, 109
Carlsbad, **14**
Carmel (-by-the-Sea), **29**, 65, 81, 84, 101-102
Carson, Kit, 127
Carson, William, 92, 93
Carson House, 92, **93**

Cascade Mountains, 10, 93
cattle, 36-37, **37**
Central Pacific Railroad Company, 50
Central Valley, 11, 13, 30, 73, 74, 96
Chamberlain, Owen, 127
Chandler, Raymond, 127
Channel Islands, 12
Chaplin, Charlie, 86, **87**, 127, **127**
Chavez, Cesar, 62, 127, **127**
child labor law, 57
Chinatown, **27**, 99
Chinese, in California, 50-51, 85
chronology, 123-126
citrus industry, 103
City Hall, Los Angeles, 105
Civil War, 49, 80
Clear Lake, 13
Clemens, Samuel (Mark Twain), 80, 94
climate, 14-15, 114
Coast Ranges, 10, 11, 14, 26
Colorado River, 73
coastlines, 12, **12**, 31
Columbia, 95, 122
communication, 77, 118
computer-related industries, 70, **70**, 98
conservation, 18-19, 31
constitution, state, 67
Coolbrith, Ina, 81
Corbett, Gentleman Jim, 127
Coronado Island, 107
Costa Mesa, **83**, 84
counties, map of, **137**
counties, number of, 68, 116
Cranston, Alan Macgregor, 127
Crocker, Charles, 50, 97
Crocker Art Museum, 97
crops, 117
dams, 74
dates, important, 123-126
De Mille, Cecil B., 128
Death Valley, **8-9**, 11, 14, 15, 103, **104**, 121, **138**
depressions, 50, 57-58, 81
deserts, 14, 16, 103-104, **104**
Deukmejian, George, Jr., 65, 128

Didion, Joan, 82, 128
Disney, Walt, 87, 128, **128**
Disneyland, 106, 122, **122**
distances, greatest, 112
Donner Party, 38
Douglas, Donald Wills, 128
Drake, Sir Francis, 32, **32**
Duncan, Isadora, 128, **128**
Dust Bowl era, 58, **58**
earthquakes, 19-21, **20**, 54-55, **55**, 56
Eastwood, Clint, 65, 128
economy, 7, 50, 56-57, 117-118
education, 68-69, 116-117
Eel River, 13
El Camino Real, 34
El Capitan, **18**, 89
El Pueblo de Los Angeles, 121
electoral votes, 116
ethnic groups, 24-25, 30, 33-34, 48, 50-51, 59
Eu, March Kong Fong, 128
Eureka, 59, 92, **93**
explorers, 31-33
Farallon Islands, 12
farming and farmland, **6**, 7, 11, 71-74
fault lines, 20-21
Feather River, 13
Feinstein, Dianne, 128, **128**
Ferlinghetti, Lawrence, 82, 128
fine arts, 82-84
First Church of Christ, Scientist, Berkeley, 84
fish, 16, 31, 76, 115
fish, state, 109
Fishermen's Wharf, Monterey, 101, **101**
Fisherman's Wharf, San Francisco, 99
fishing, 76, **76**
flag, state, **108**, 109
flower, state, **108**, 109
Folsom Dam, 74
Fontana, 70
food-processing industry, 71
forests, 16, **17**, 18-19, 75, 103
forty-niners, 43-45, **44**
442nd Regiment, 59

freeways, 28, 63, 76-77, **105**
Frémont, John Charles, 39, 47, 128, **128**
Fresno, 26, 82, 84
Friant Dam, 74
fruit, 56, **56**
Gali, Francisco, 32-33
Gálvez, Don José de, 33
Garden City, 84
Gardner, John William, 128
Garland, Judy, 129, **129**
geography, 10-13, 111-114
Ghirardelli Square, **99**
Giannini, Amadeo Peter, 56
Gilroy, 71
gold and gold mining, 31, 42-47, **44**, 48, 74-75, 95
Gold Rush, 18, 42-47, **43**, **44**, **45**, 48, 51, 80, 85, 96
Golden Gate Bridge, 77, **90-91**, 97
Golden Gate Park, 99, **99**
Golden Hind, ship, 32, **32**
government, 67-68, 115-116
Governor's Mansion, Sacramento, 97
governors of California, 132
Grapes of Wrath, The, 24, 58, 81
grasses and grasslands, 16, **17**, 37, **37**
Griffith, D. W., 86, 129
Hale, George Ellery, 129
Harbor Freeway, **105**
Hart, William S., 86
Harte, Bret, 80, 129
Hayakawa, S. I., 27, 129, **129**
Hearst, William Randolph, 102, 129, **129**
Hearst Castle, 102, 121
highest point, 11, 111
highways, 28, 63, 76-77
highways, major, map of, **136**
Hispanics, 24-25, 27, 65
historic sites and landmarks, 120-121
Hollyhock House, 84
Hollywood, 57, 77, **78-79**, 105, 122, **122**
Hollywood Bowl, **78-79**, 86, 106

Honey Lake, 13
Hopkins, Mark, 50
hot-air ballooning, 89, **89**
Humboldt Bay, 59
Huntington, Collis Potter, 50, 129
Hupa people, 30
immigrants, 48, 50-51, 57, 65
Imperial Dam, 74
Imperial Valley, 73
Indians, 24, 30-31, 34-36, 37, 82, 103, 104
industry, 7, 56-57, 70-71, 117-118
Innocents Abroad, 80
Inyo National Forest, 121
irrigation, 72-73, 104
Jackson, Helen Hunt, 129
Japanese Americans, 59
Jeffers, (John) Robinson, 129
Johnson, Earvin "Magic," 88
Johnson, Hiram, 57
Joshua Tree National Monument, 104, **104**, 121
Judah, Theodore Dehone, 49-50, **50**, 96
Kaiser Shipyards, 60
Kearney, Steven Watts, 39
Keaton, Buster, 86, 129
Kerouac, Jack, 82, 129, **129**
Kings Canyon, 95
Klamath Mountains, 10
Klamath River, 13
Knott's Berry Farm, 122
La Brea Tar Pits, 121
Laguna Beach, 106
Lake Arrowhead, 103
Lake Manzanita, **94**
Lake Merritt, 97, **98**
Lake Shasta, 13, 74
Lake Tahoe, 13, **13**, 15, 94
lakes, 13, 112
Lange, Dorothea, 130
Lassen Volcanic National Park, **11**, 94, **94**
Lawrence, Ernest Orlando, 130
Lewis, Sinclair, 81
libraries, 68, 119
literature, 80-82

Livermore Valley, 96
logging industry, 18-19, **74**, 75
Lombard Street, San Francisco, **99**
London, Jack, 81, 130, **130**
Long Beach, 20, 26, 56, 75
Los Angeles, 19-20, **25**, 26, 27, 50-51, 57, 59, 60, 61, 63, **63**, 64, **65**, 70, 72, 76, 77, 83, 84, 105-106, **105**
Los Angeles Aqueduct, 73
Los Angeles Coliseum, 64, **65**
Los Angeles Times, 77
lowest point, 11, 112
Lummis, Charles Fletcher, 130
MacDonald, Ross, 130
Mad River, 13
Maidu people, 30
Malibu, 105
Mammoth Pool Reservoir, 95
manifest destiny, 38-39
manufacturing, 70-71, 117
maps of California:
    counties, **137**
    highways, major, **136**
    political, **135**
    population density, **136**
    precipitation, **136**
    products, principal, **136**
    topography, **137**
maps of United States:
    political, **133**
    topographical, **133**
Marineland, 122
Maritime Museum, San Diego, 107
McCloud River, 13
McMillan, Edwin, 130
McPherson, Aimee Semple, 130, **130**
Mendocino, 93
Merced River, 13, **18**, 95
Merriam, Frank F., 58
mestizos, 33-34
Mexican-American War, 39
Mexico, 12, 31, 33, 36-37, 38, 39
Mills College, 98
minerals and mining, 18, 42-47, **44**, 48, 50, 74-75, 117

Building sand castles at Pacific Beach

missionaries, 33, 34-36
missions, 33, 34-36, 82, 84
Mojave Desert, 10, 83
Mojave people, 30
Monroe, Marilyn, 130, **130**
Monterey, 38, 101, **101**
Monterey Bay, 12, 13, 33, 89
Mother Lode Country, 46, 95
motto, state, 109
Mount Lassen, 94, **94**
Mount Shasta, 93
Mount Whitney, 11, 95
mountains, 7, 10
movies and motion picture
   industry, 10, 56, 57, 61, 65, 77,
   86-87, **87**, 106
Muir, John, 10, 18, 19, 95, 130,
   130
Muir Woods, 97, 121
Mulholland, William, 72, 73
Museum of Contemporary Art,
   Los Angeles, 106, **106**
museums, 118-119
music, 85-86
Nahl, Charles, 83
Napa Valley, 71, **73**, 89, **89**, 96
Natural History Museum, San
   Diego, **119**

natural resources, 117
Nevada, 12, 50
New Spain, 31, 35
Newport Beach, 106
newspapers, 77
nickname, state, 16, 17, 109
Nixon, Richard Milhous, 64, 130
Noguchi, Isamu, 83, 84
Norris, Frank, 80
Oakland, 26, 60, 77, 97, **98**
Oakland Museum, 97
Octopus, The, 80-81
oil industry, 19, 56, **56**, 75, **75**
Oklahomans, 58, **58**
Old Town Heritage Park, San
   Diego, **52-53**
Olvera Street, Los Angeles, **25**
Olympic Games, 15, 64, **65**, 94
Orange County, 106
Orange County Performing Arts
   Center, 84
Orange County Register, 77
Oregon, 12, 16, 38, 39, 59, 75
Oroville Dam, 74
Owens River Valley, 72, 73
Pacific Beach, **141**
Pacific coast, **2-3**, 14, 16, 26
Pacific Ocean, 12, 26, 38, 39

Palace of the Legion of Honor,
   99
Palm Canyon, **113**
Palm Springs, 51, 104
Palo Alto, 98
Pasadena, 14, 51, 76
Patton, George, 131, **131**
Pauling, Linus, 131
Pebble Beach, 89, **89**
people of California, **22-23**,
   24-28
people of California, important,
   126-132
Pereira, William, 84
performing arts, 85-86, 119-120
Pickford, Mary, 86
pioneers, 7, 38-39, **38**
Pit River, 13
Pittsburg, 70
plants, wild, 16, 114-115
Play It As It Lays, 82
Pomo people, 30
Pony Express, 49, **49**, 96
population figures, 24, 25, 26,
   30, 48, 51, 57, 60, 110-111, **136**
   (map)
Porciuncula River, 33
Portolá, Gaspar de, 33

ports, 77
Portsmouth Square, 49
precipitation, 14, 15, **136** (map)
products, principal, 117, **136** (map)
prospectors, **40-41**, 95
race riots, 51, 61-62
railroads, 48-50, **50**, 57, 77
Reagan, Ronald, 63, 64, 131, **131**
recreation, 120
Redding, 92
Redwood City, 98
Redwood Highway, 123
Redwood National Park, 92
redwood trees, 15, 16, **17**, 18-19,
    92, 97, **108**
representatives, U.S., number of,
    116
Ribbon Falls, 123
Richmond, 60
Richmond-San Rafael Bridge,
    77, 97
rivers, 11, 13, 112
Riverside, 103
rock, state, 109
Rodia, Simon, 83
Rogers, Will, 24
Roosevelt, Franklin D., 59
Russian River, 13, 93, 96
Russians, in California, 37
Sacramento, 26, 42-43, 47, 49,
    66, 77, 96-97, **96**
Sacramento History Center, 97
Sacramento River, 11, **11**, 13, 74,
    74
Sacramento River delta, **6, 11**
Sacramento Valley, 11, 36, 73
St. Joseph, Missouri, 49
Salinas, 81, **81**
Salinas River, 13
Salton Sea, 73
San Andreas Fault, 21, **21**
San Carlos Borromeo del Rio
    Carmelo, **29**, 84, 121
San Diego, 15, 26, 33, 34, 36,
    52-53, 59, **76**, 77, 97, 107, **107**,
    119
San Diego Bay, 12, 31, 33
San Diego de Alcalá, **35**, **84**, 121
San Diego Zoo, 107, 123

San Francisco, **4**, 14, 16, 18, 20,
    21, 26, **27**, 32, 33, 42-43, 47, 48,
    51, 54-55, **55**, 57, 59, 60, 63, 70,
    77, 82, 85, 97-100, **99**, **100**, 123
San Francisco Bay, 12, 26, 33, 97
San Francisco Chronicle, 77
San Francisco-Oakland Bay
    Bridge, 77
San Gabriel Archangel, 84
San Joaquin River, 11, 13
San Joaquin Valley, 11, 73, 75,
    103
San Jose, 26, 33, 47, 98
San Juan Capistrano, 121
San Luis Obispo, 34, 86
San Pedro, 60
San Simeon, 102
Santa Ana, 26
Santa Ana River, 13
Santa Barbara, 102
Santa Barbara Islands, 12
Santa Clara, 98
Santa Clara River, 13
Santa Clara Valley, 33
Santa Cruz, 86, 101, **116**
Santa Lucia Range, 13
Santa Monica, 51, 63
Saroyan, William, 82, 131
Sausalito, 97
schools, 60, 68-69, 116-117
Sea World, 107
Seaborg, Glenn Theodore,
    131
Selznick, David, 131
Sequoia National Park, 95
sequoias, giant, 16, **17**, 19, 95
Serra, Father Junipero, 33, 34,
    35, 36, 84, 102, 131
settlers, 24, 33-34, 36, 37, 38-39,
    38
Seventeen-Mile Drive, 89, 101,
    101
Shasta Dam, 74, **74**
shipyards, 59-60
Sierra Club, 19
Sierra Madre Mountains, 10
Sierra Nevada Mountains, 10,
    11, 13, 15, 19, 38, 39, 46, 83,
    94-95

Signal Hill, 56
Silicon Valley, 70, **70**, 98
Sinclair, Upton, 58, 81
smog, **63**
soil, 72, 96
song, state, 110
Sonoma, 39
Sonoma County, 96
Sonoma Valley, 36
Sonora Desert, 104
Soule, Frank, 48
South America, 31
Spaniards, in California, 31-36
sports, 88-89, 120
Squaw Valley, 15, 94
Stanford, Leland, 50, 131
Stanford University, 69, **69**, 98
Stanislaus River, 13
State Capitol, Sacramento, **66**,
    123
State Indian Museum,
    Sacramento, 97
statehood, 47, 109
Steinbeck, John, 24, 58, 81, **81**,
    131
Sterling, George, 81
Stockton, 77
Stockton, Robert, 39
Strauss, Levi, 46, 131, **131**
Studebaker, John, 46
Sullivan, John, 46
Sutter, John, 36, 42, **43**, 47, 131
Sutter's Fort, 97
Tehachapi Mountains, 10, 26
telegraph, 49
temperatures, 14-15, 114
Temple (Black), Shirley, 131, **131**
Texas, 38, 39, 58
theater, 85, 86
Tiburon, 97
Time of Your Life, The, 82
topography, 112-114, **133**, (U.S.
    map), **137** (California map)
Torrance, 70
Tortilla Flat, 81
Transamerica Pyramid, 84, **84**
transcontinental railroad, 49-50,
    50
transportation, 76-77, 118

tree, state, **108**, 109
trees, 7, 15-16, **17**, 114
Trinity River, 13
Truckee, 94
Tuolumne River, 13
Twain, Mark (Samuel Clemens), 80, 94
unemployment, 50, 57-58, 61
United Nations, 60
U.S. Highway 101, 92, 123
Universal Studios, 106
universities, 62-63, 69, 116-117
University of California at Berkeley, 62, 63, 69
University of California at Davis, 72

University of California at Los Angeles, 88
University of California at Riverside, 72
University of California at Santa Cruz, **116**
University of Southern California, 69, 88
Vallejo, 47, 60
Vallejo, Mariano Guadalupe, 37, 132
Vizcaino, Sebastián, 33
voting qualifications, 116
Warren, Earl, 60, 132, **132**
Washington (state), 59, 75
Watts, Los Angeles, 61-62, **62**, 82

Watts Towers, 83, **83**
Wayne, John, 132, **132**
weapons industry, 71
weather, 14-15, 114
Weinberger, Caspar, 132
Weston, Edward, 83, 132
White Mountains, 16
wine industry, **73**, 96, 123
World War II, 59-60
Wright, Frank Lloyd, 84
Yerba Buena, 33
Yokut people, 30
Yosemite National Park, **18**, 19, 89, 95
Yosemite Valley, 18, 83
Yuma people, 30, 34

Picture Identifications

Front cover: The skyline of the San Francisco financial district forms a background for Victorian houses on Steiner Street
Back cover: Rhododendrons and redwoods in fog-shrouded Redwoods State Park
Pages 2-3: Rocky Pacific coastline
Page 6: Sacramento River delta farmland
Pages 8-9: Death Valley sand dunes
Pages 22-23: Montage of California residents
Page 29: Mission San Carlos Borromeo, Carmel
Pages 40-41: Prospectors on their way to the gold fields
Pages 52-53: Old Town Heritage Park, San Diego
Page 66: The State Capitol in Sacramento
Pages 78-79: The Hollywood Bowl
Page 78 (inset): A windsurfer
Pages 90-91: The Golden Gate Bridge
Page 91 (inset): Laguna Beach
Page 108: Montage showing the state flag, the state tree (California redwood), the state mineral (native gold), the state flower (golden poppy), and the state bird (California valley quail)

About the Author

R. Conrad Stein was born and grew up in Chicago. He began writing professionally shortly after graduating from the University of Illinois. He is the author of many books, articles, and short stories written for young readers. Mr. Stein first saw California as a young marine stationed at bases at San Diego and Oceanside. To prepare for this book, he traveled the length and breadth of the Golden State, stopping often to talk to the people. He concluded that California's unique blend of beauty and energy makes the state a magnet for the world. Mr. Stein now lives in Chicago with his wife and their daughter Janna.

Picture Acknowledgments

H. Armstrong Roberts: © J. Messerschmidt: Front cover
© **Bob and Ira Spring:** Back cover
Photri: Pages 44 (right), 87 (all six pictures), 105 (right), 122 (left), 131 (Patton and Reagan);
© Edmond Van Hoorick: Pages 2-3, 37, 90-91; © C.W. Biedel, M.D.: Pages 8-9, 93, 101 (right);
© Larry Allan: Page 107; © Len Rue, Jr.: Page 108 (bottom right)
Root Resources: © James Blank: Pages 4, 14 (right), 25 (left), 26 (right), 63 (left), 69 (left), 73
(left), 89 (left), 91 (inset), 101 (left), 141; © Pat Vine: Page 12 (right); © Bert Van Bork: Page 20;
© Jan Bannan: Page 32 (left); © Kenneth W. Fink: Page 74 (left); © Wanda Christl: Pages 100
(left), 102
Journalism Services: © H. Rick Bamman: Page 5; © Dirk Gallian Photography: Page 14 (left);
© Mark Snyder Photography: Page 23 (top left), 84 (left); © Rene Sheret: Pages 26 (left), 63
(right), 78-79, 83 (left), 106; © Dave Brown: Page 66
Marilyn Gartman Agency: © Herwig: Pages 6, 11 (right); © Spencer Grant: Page 23 (right)
© **Lynn M. Stone:** Pages 11 (left), 94
© **SuperStock International:** Pages 12 (left), 17 (top right), 18 (both pictures), 27 (left), 35,
52-53, 99 (left), 100 (right), 113, 119
© **Lee Foster:** Pages 13, 17 (bottom), 23 (middle left), 25 (right), 29, 43 (right), 45 (both
pictures), 50 (left and inset), 70 (both pictures), 73 (right), 74 (right), 81 (left), 83 (right), 84
(right), 89 (right), 98 (both pictures), 108 (bottom left), 116, 138
Nawrocki Stock Photo: © Jeff Apoian: Pages 17, (top left), 78 (inset), 108 (trees); © Christina
N. Mackenzie: Page 22 (top left); © Price Deratzian: Page 22 (top right); © Jim Wright: Pages
22 (middle left), 99 (bottom right); © J. Steere: Page 22 (bottom left); © Mukul Roy: Page 23
(bottom left); © Mike J. Howell: Page 65 (both pictures), © Steve Vidler: Pages 96, 104 (left),
122 (right); © Larry Stevens: Page 108 (top right)
Image Bank: © Barrie Rokeach: Pages 21, 75
© **Mary E. Messenger:** Page 22 (middle right and bottom right)
Cameramann International Ltd.: Pages 27 (right), 56 (both pictures), 69 (right), 76, 105 (left)
Historical Pictures Service, Inc., Chicago: Pages 32 (right), 38, 40-41, 43 (left), 44 (inset), 49,
50 (right), 55 (both pictures), 58 (left), 126 (Bierce), 127 (Burbank)
Wide World Photos: Pages 58 (right), 62, 81 (right), 126 (Adams), 127 (Bradley, Chaplin, and
Chavez), 128 (all four pictures), 129 (all four pictures), 130 (all four pictures), 131 (Strauss and
Temple), 132 (both pictures)
© **Anke Van Aardenne:** Page 99 (top right)
Odyssey Productions: © Robert Frerck: Page 104 (right)
Len W. Meents: Maps on pages 93, 94, 96, 102, 104, 106, 136
Courtesy Flag Research Center, Winchester, Massachusetts 01890: Flag on page 108